71421

W9-CMP-577

Congo to Cape

CONGO TO CAPE

Early Portuguese Explorers

by

ERIC AXELSON

Edited by George Woodcock

BARNES & NOBLE

BOOKS

10 East 53d St., New York 10022
(a division of Harper & Row Publishers, Inc.)

Published in the U.S.A. 1973 by
HARPER & ROW PUBLISHERS LTD
BARNES & NOBLE IMPORT DIVISION
Printed in Great Britain
All rights reserved

ISBN 06–490252–8

Contents

Illustrations

PLATES

9

MAPS

Preface

Sailing from Portugal on his earliest voyage of exploration in 1482, Diogo Cão was the first European to explore the west coast of Central Africa, from Cape Santa Catarina, a few miles south of the equator, to a point beyond Cape Cross in South-West Africa. In the course of his second voyage in 1485–6 he sailed up the estuary of the River Congo, and made contact with the king of the Congo people, who ruled over the largest and most powerful kingdom in that region. Bartolomeu Dias continued Cão's explorations; in 1488 he actually rounded the southern extremity of the African continent, and opened the sea route from Europe into the Indian Ocean. These were remarkable feats for which—outside Portugal—Cão and Dias have received less than the recognition which is their due. The primary intent of this book is to outline the positive achievements of the two explorers.

There are few contemporary records relating to Cão and Dias, and one is forced to glean much of one's information from chronicles written in the sixteenth century and in some cases perhaps distorted by political considerations, from near-contemporary maps which usually presented second- or third-hand knowledge which had passed through the hands of commercial spies before it was incorporated in charts drawn in countries outside Portugal, and from the stone pillars or *padrões* which the explorers themselves erected on prominent points during their voyages. These pillars, cut from Portuguese limestone, served as landmarks; on each of them the Portuguese King's coat of arms and an appropriate inscription asserted his country's rights to the seas around and the adjacent lands; the cross surmounting each pillar proclaimed that the exploration was being carried out in the name of the Christian religion. In the following narrative the present writer's discovery of the farthest *padrão* erected by Bartolomeu Dias and his establishment of the actual sites of others of these monuments will of necessity find its place.

My interest in Portuguese exploration began when, as a schoolboy, I spent nearly every holiday on board a coasting vessel, marvelling at the beauties and dangers of the South African shoreline, and also at the number of Portuguese names that adorned its charts. My study of the background to those names began seriously one day in 1935 when I entered the room of Professor Leo Fouché, Head of the Department of History at the University of Witwatersrand, in Johannesburg. I had been given the funds to devote three years to historical research, and up to this point I had been delving into the history of early British colonization in Natal. I proposed to continue this work in England. Professor Fouché looked at me over his spectacles. 'A very interesting subject,' he remarked, 'but before the British reached Natal, the Dutch were there; and before the Dutch, the Portuguese. It was the Portuguese who gave the place its name, after all. Portuguese castaways were walking through Natal a hundred years before the first Dutchman settled at the Cape of Good Hope. There is history for you—the Portuguese period in the history of southern Africa. And up to now it is almost untouched!'

Professor Fouché went on to tell how the Cape government towards the end of the last century had sent G. M. Theal, the most prolific of all writers on South African history, to Europe so that he could research into the Portuguese period. Theal gathered enough material to publish nine volumes of documents and of extracts from chronicles about the Portuguese in southern Africa—but he never reached Portugal itself.

'Think of Bartolomeu Dias,' Professor Fouché continued. 'We all know that he was the first European to round Africa and reach the Indian Ocean. But where did he turn back? We know that somewhere near where he turned he put up a stone cross. But no one has found it. Why don't you go to Portugal and look for the clues? Why don't you find that cross?'

There was no resisting such an argument. I went to Portugal, though first I spent some months in Johannesburg learning as much of the rudiments of Portuguese as I could from the local experts and working my way through the documents collected and published by Theal; after that I spent almost a year reading in the British Museum and in the India Office Library, attending seminars presided over by Arthur Percival Newton at the Institute of Historical Research, and listening to Professor Edgar Prestage who had just published *The Portuguese Pioneers* in which he frankly declared his admiration for the crusading zeal of these voyagers while admitting the strength of their desire for material gain.

In Portugal I spent most of my time in the Arquivo Nacional da Tôrre do Tombo, searching for documents about early Portuguese contacts with southern Africa. The great mass of the papers of the House of Guinea and India had perished when the castle of São Jorge, in which they were stored, burnt down after the Lisbon earthquake of 1755. Those that had been saved were preserved in a wing of the old convent of São Bento; they were badly catalogued, and the conditions under which one worked in the 1930s were difficult and discouraging. The walls were thick and the windows small and deeply recessed, so that the light was poor and the reading room was open only from 11 a.m. to 4 p.m. since, for fear of fire, the director refused to allow electric light to be installed. When the attendants went into the basement to search for documents, they had to carry candles, and the records themselves were in such condition that the readers found it necessary every now and again to shake from their laps the bookworms that were visibly eating away the papers and parchments. (In all fairness I must say that when I returned in 1949, conditions were somewhat improved; the stacks had been fumigated and the assistants had been issued with electric torches.) I was also able to make use of the splendidly organized Arquivo Histórico Colonial (now known as the Arquivo Histórico Ultramarino) but this contained no documents earlier than the 1580s. I also found that for general reading on exploration and colonization there was no library that could rival that of the Sociedade de Geografia de Lisboa. On the floor below the library was the Society's museum, and here I saw the relics of the explorers, and especially the one complete *padrão*, erected by Diogo Cão, which came back to his homeland with its message intact. More than anything else, the sight of that monument encouraged me to search for the missing *padrões* of Cão's successor Bartolomeu Dias when I returned home from my studies in 1938.

In view of the loss of all the original documents relating to the voyages of Cão and Dias, none of which came to light during my researches in the Arquivo Nacional da Tôrre do

Tombo, I had to rely heavily on the chronicles which were written in the sixteenth and the very last years of the fifteenth centuries, and published usually some time afterwards. There was—as will become evident—other information, and especially that provided in maps drawn outside Portugal during the years immediately following the voyages of Cão and Dias, but it was at best fragmentary and often dubious in origin or significance, so that it would have been difficult for me to carry out my searches without the essential narrative framework which the chronicles provided. These and other sources are listed in the bibliography, but before I begin my own account it may be useful to mention at least the most important of them.

Rui de Pina started his *Croniqua del Rey Dom Joham II* soon after his appointment as Portuguese chronicler-in-chief in 1497 and completed it early in the sixteenth century; it was not published until 1792. It was used by Garcia de Resende, whose *Vida e Feitos del Rey João segundo* was completed in 1533 and published in 1545. João de Barros, who had been captain of Mina and treasurer of the House of Guinea and India, completed the first books of his *Da Asia* in 1539, but they were not published until 1552. He was a fine stylist, but not so accurate as Fernão Lopes de Castanheda, whose *História do descobrimento e conquista da India pelos portugueses* was published in 1551, but Castanheda unfortunately dismissed the period before Vasco da Gama in a few paragraphs. Antonio Galvão was equally brief in his *Tratado . . . de todos os descombrimentos . . .* (1563).

Most valuable in any consideration of the voyages of Cão and Dias is the route-book of Duarte Pacheco Pereira, who accompanied Azambuja when he founded the Portuguese fortress at Mina on the Gold Coast in 1482 and came to know the Guinea coast intimately, being rescued there by

Dias in 1488 when the latter was returning home from the discovery of the Cape of Good Hope. Pacheco Pereira also explored the western Atlantic. Early in the sixteenth century he sailed to India and gained such glory that on his return to Portugal King Manuel ordered a public thanksgiving in his honour. Between 1505 and 1508 he wrote his *Esmeraldo de Situ Orbis* which he described as a 'book of seamanship and cosmography'. This rutter* outlined the sea routes to be followed by Portuguese ships, especially those proceeding to the Indies, and described the appearance of the land, noting prominent features and harbours, providing soundings, bearings and latitudes, and often mentioning the actions of the early voyagers. Another important rutter, also dating from the early sixteenth century, is that attached to the *Livro de marinharia* of João de Lisboa.

Hardly less important are the near-contemporary charts to which I have already referred, but the most important of these are described in Chapter II, while some of them are illustrated. Primary sources of lesser importance and valuable secondary sources are listed in the bibliography at the end of this book.

* O.E.D. 'ruttier': 'a set of instructions for finding one's course at sea; a marine guide to the routes, tides, etc.'

Acknowledgements

Several years ago (just how many I am ashamed to admit) Professor George Woodcock wrote to me from Vancouver and inquired whether I might perhaps be interested in writing a biography of Bartolomeu Dias for Messrs Faber and Faber's Great Travellers series. I was naturally excited at this offer, knowing the reputation both of the publishers and of Professor Woodcock. My interest in the subject stemmed in general from lengthy researches into the history of Portuguese exploration and colonization in southern Africa, and more particularly from the discovery of fragments of two stone landmarks raised by Dias on the south African coast. I had, however, reluctantly to tell Professor Woodcock that insufficient source material had survived the centuries to enable an entire volume to be devoted to Dias alone. I suggested that its scope be extended to include also an account of the voyages of Diogo Cão (about whose life there is also distressingly little known). The proposal was accepted, and whenever opportunity permitted I buried myself in the sources. But my nose was too close to the contemporary manuscripts, to early maps and twentieth-century charts, to pilot-books both ancient and modern. The result was an incompletely digested hotchpotch. I am deeply indebted to Professor Woodcock for having breathed life into this material, and for having been responsible for a readable book.

ACKNOWLEDGEMENTS

For the photographs shown in Plates I and III, I acknowledge my indebtedness to Dr. Pietro Puliatti, director of the Biblioteca Estense, and Cav. Uff. Umberto Orlandini, Modena; Plate II to the Board of Trustees of the British Museum; Plate IV to Prof. Armando Cortesão and Commander Avelino Teixeira da Mota, authors of *Portugaliae Monumenta Cartographica*; Plate V to Mr. Michael Teague; Plate VII, Mr. E. Rabinow; Plate X, the Director of the Library, Academia das Ciências de Lisboa and St. Horácio de Souza Novais.

I am grateful also to Neil Hyslop for drawing the three maps.

I

The Portuguese Pioneers

IT was no accident that Portugal became the first European country in modern times to explore and colonize beyond the seas. Her medieval wars of independence against Leon and Castile, and her campaigns against the Moors in the Iberian peninsula, had encouraged the growth of a national spirit by the time—in the middle of the twelfth century—Portugal attained what are essentially her present frontiers. Bounded by unfriendly and often actively hostile Spanish kingdoms and Muslim principalities, Portugal was forced to look to the sea not merely for communication with the rest of Christendom, but also for essential trade: the export of salt and oil, of wine and cork, and the import of most of the manufactured goods her people needed. Moreover, her pastures and her cultivated lands were infertile, and the sea provided necessary food. Her fishermen became consummate seamen, and out of their ranks emerged the crews of ships that sailed in the Middle Ages to the farthest parts of north-western Europe and of the Mediterranean.

An important event in Portuguese naval history took place in 1317 when King Dinis engaged, as his admiral, Emanuel Passagno of Genoa, then the leading naval power of the Mediterranean. Passagno was accompanied, according to the terms of his contract, by 'twenty men of Genoa, experienced in the sea, qualified as masters and pilots'; the

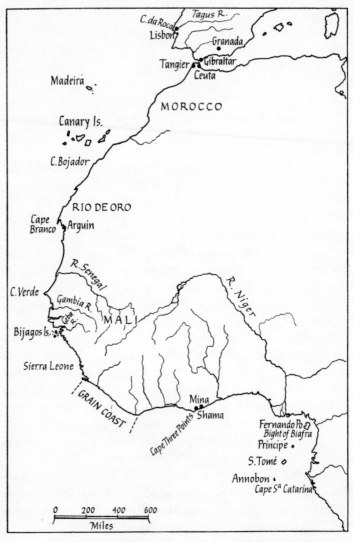

1. West Africa coastline, Ceuta to Cape Santa Catarina

party may also have included cartographers and designers. With such an injection of experience and skill, and with the King's encouragement of ship-building, Portugal soon developed a formidable navy. Other maritime activity intensified, and the Atlantic became more than ever a medium of communication to the Portuguese and a source of life to their country. Their attention began to turn southward. They swept the Moorish galleys from the coast of Algarve and sent an expedition to the Canaries.

Portuguese expansion overseas began in 1415 with the conquest of Ceuta in Morocco by King João I, a campaign of which little would be known if it were not for the writings of the fifteenth-century chronicler Gomes Eanes de Zurara, who tells us that the king was disturbed by the memory of Christian blood shed during his wars against his co-religionists of Castile, and thought that the best means of penance would be 'to wash his hands in the blood of infidels'. Undoubtedly the crusading urge was strong in King João, but, as Professor Edgar Prestage has pointed out, there are other possible reasons for his expedition, such as the need to repress piracy in the Straits of Gibraltar and the fact that Ceuta was an important emporium, the terminus of a trans-Saharan caravan route by which gold was brought to the Mediterranean coast.

In fact, the real inspirer of the expedition to Ceuta appears to have been the royal treasurer, João Afonso de Alenquer, who appreciated how much profit would come from the capture of the city, not only in actual loot, but also from piratical attacks on Muslim ships passing through the Straits and from controlling the gold trade. On the last subject his knowledge was doubtless considerable, for Arab geographers and Jewish traders had already informed Europeans of the nature of the trans-Saharan trade, which dealt not only with gold, but also in ivory, negro slaves, and the false pepper from the west African coast known as malagueta.

Such information was often incorporated in exotic accounts of the negro empire of Mali to the south of the Sahara, whose ruler, Mansa Musa, had set out in 1324 on a famous pilgrimage to Mecca. Before this king's horse marched five hundred slaves, each carrying a staff of gold, and in Cairo he is said to have distributed nearly a hundred camel-loads of gold, each weighing approximately 300 pounds; so lavish, indeed, were his spending and his gifts that in the Levant the market value of gold slumped appreciably. The kingdom from which this wealth was derived was centred on the headwaters of the Niger, and it stretched all the way from the Atlantic coast, where it reached north of the Senegal and south of the Gambia Rivers, to the middle reaches of the Niger, and from north of Timbuktu, which became the main *entrepôt* of the gold trade, to below Gao.

Mansa Musa died in 1332, and only seven years later Angelino Dulcert (or Dalorto) drew in Mallorca a world-map on which figures a picture of the 'Rex Melly' who dominated the interior of west Africa; a road marked through the Atlas mountains was described as running to the Land of the Negroes. Later, in 1375, another Mallorcan map-maker, Abraham Cresques, elaborated on the same theme, showing the king, crowned and seated on a throne, with a sceptre over one shoulder, while in his other hand he held an orb of gold. The adjoining legend declares: 'This negro king is called Musa Mali, lord of the negroes of Guinea. So abundant is the gold which is found in his country that he is the richest and most noble king in all the land.' Again, the road through the Atlas mountains is shown, with the indication that it is used by 'the merchants who travel to the land of the negroes of Guinea'. These maps, or copies of them, were doubtless known to the Portuguese court.

Some time before the expedition against Ceuta, João Afonso sent an agent to that city; his ostensible mission was to buy slaves, but his real intent was to establish the extent of the gold trade. On his return he not only gave an enticing report of the riches of Ceuta, but he also exclaimed on the beauty of the city, with its crenellated walls and massive citadels, its commanding buildings, its fruitful orchards and its gardens of delight. Inland from the city, and to the south-west on the slopes facing the Atlantic, stretched fertile wheatfields. Portugal was desperately short of wheat.

At first João Afonso failed to convince his ruler of the wisdom of embarking on an adventure against Ceuta, so he presented its advantages to the three older sons of King João I and Philippa of Lancaster (daughter of John of Gaunt whose marriage had sealed in 1386 the Treaty of Windsor between England and Portugal). These three princes, Duarte, Pedro and Henrique (later to become celebrated as Prince Henry the Navigator), had all come of age, and they nurtured the chivalrous wish of young aristo-crats of their age to be knighted on the field of battle. This meant that Portugal, having signed its peace treaty with Castile in 1411, must now seek enemies beyond the bounds of Iberia.

The princes' arguments finally persuaded King João to re-examine Afonso's proposal, but before making a final decision he reconnoitred cautiously, sending two galleys on a bogus diplomatic mission to Sicily, ostensibly to demand the hand of its Queen for his second son Pedro. While one of the galleys sheltered in the harbour of Ceuta, the ambassador assessed the defences of the city, and the captain found suitable beaches for landing. Once he himself was convinced of the feasibility of the operation, João had no difficulty in persuading the members of his council of state, whose agreement was motivated by weighty considerations of strategy.

For it was with good reason that the old chronicler Zurara called Ceuta the key to the Mediterranean. The prizes to be gained from Portuguese occupation of this Moroccan fortress were many and great. Such occupation, as the modern Portuguese historian Vitorino Magalhães Godinho has pointed out, would guarantee the Christian kingdoms of Iberia, and especially the Algarve coast, from Moorish invasion, and it would secure the Portuguese lines of communication with the Christian realms of Italy and north-western Europe. Besides safeguarding the passage of Portuguese shipping through the Straits of Gibraltar, it would provide a base both for active commercial and political penetration into North Africa and also for piracy against Muslim shipping and a bridgehead for the later conquest of Morocco. While facilitating the interruption of reinforcements from Morocco to the surviving Muslim kingdom of Granada in Spain, it would also prevent any move by Portugal's Christian competitor, Castile, into north-west Africa. Finally, and perhaps of most immediate importance to King João and his advisers, it would dominate the northern terminus of the trans-Saharan trade route.

To dissimulate the reasons for his preparations and conceal the real goal of attack, King João dispatched yet another bogus diplomatic mission, this time to throw down an empty challenge to the Duke of Burgundy, whose subjects had been plundering Portuguese ships. Meanwhile, the expedition was assembled with dispatch and enthusiasm, as Zurara recounted in his *Cronica de Ceuta*:

'The fervour was so great that the people worked at

nothing else, some in cleaning their arms, others in making biscuits and salting meat, others in repairing ships and arranging crews, so that nothing should be wanting in time of need . . . All along the riverside lay ships, great and small, on which by day and night caulkers and others were working to repair their defects; near them lay many slaughtered oxen and cows, and many men were engaged in skinning and cutting up and salting them, while others packed them in barrels and boats for the voyage. The fishermen and their wives were salting various kinds of fish, and every free bit of ground was covered with them. The officials of the mint never had their hammers quiet by day or night, so that if a man shouted among the furnaces, he could hardly be understood; and the coopers had no small toil in making and repairing barrels for the wine and meat and other goods, and the tailors and cloth-workers in preparing cloth and making liveries of various kinds, as his master directed, and the carpenters in packing bombards and guns and preparing all other sorts of artillery, which were many and great, and the ropemakers in making many kinds of cords for the ships.' (Translated by Edgar Prestage in *The Portuguese Pioneers*, Adam and Charles Black, London, 1933, pp. 21–2.)

Finally, in July 1415, the Portuguese armada set sail, with 20,000 men in about 200 vessels. On the 15th August Ceuta was attacked and occupied with surprising ease. The event had reverberations that were to resound through Europe and the world for many years, since it not only dispossessed the Moors of their best stronghold, but it also led to the expansion of Portugal as a trading and colonial power, and among its distant consequences were the voyages of Diogo Cão and Bartolomeu Dias.

From interrogating prisoners, from talking to the citizens

of Ceuta and the visiting traders, and from reading captured documents, Prince Henry must have learnt much about the geography of north-west Africa, and he doubtless increased this knowledge on his return to Ceuta in 1418 when the Moors attempted to recapture the city. Back in Portugal he began to devote himself to the cause of maritime exploration with that fervour which earned him the title of Prince Henry the Navigator. He used the Lagos region, in the province of Algarve, as his base of operations, which were financed largely by the militant Order of Christ, of which he was the Grand Master.

Prince Henry left no documents which declared the motives that led to his activities, but Zurara, writing possibly before the Navigator's death, listed five probable reasons. First, there was the kind of disinterested curiosity that was typical of the Renaissance; Prince Henry wished to learn about lands that lay beyond the bounds of European knowledge, which at that time extended no farther than the Canary Islands and Cape Bojador in what became the Spanish Sahara; beyond these points all was blank except for the legendary voyage of the Irish monk, St. Brendan. But Prince Henry was also moved by the hope of finding Christian ports where Portuguese vessels might find both shelter and commerce; such trade could be profitable if European competitors were discouraged and Portuguese goods were used to buy local products cheaply. A third motive, according to Zurara, sprang from Prince Henry's suspicion that the power of the Moors in Africa might be greater than had previously been supposed; common prudence demanded that one learn one's adversary's strength, and so Henry wished to reconnoitre the extent of Muslim influence in Africa.

The final motive in Prince Henry's activity—listed fifth

by Zurara—was to increase the Christian faith, and this desire was undoubtedly one of the most potent forces inspiring the great age of Portuguese imperialism from beginning to end. Linked with it is the fourth and certainly the most exotic of the motives in Zurara's list. He claims that, wishing to fight against the Muslims, Henry could find no European ally in that age when Crusades on the grand medieval scale were going out of fashion, and he hoped that in some remoter region his captains would discover a Christian prince who would join him in campaigns against the enemies of the faith.

The allusion is undoubtedly to that semi-legendary figure, Prester John. From the middle of the twelfth century Europe had been swept by rumours that in Asia there lived a powerful Christian king and priest, an adherent of the Nestorian heresy, called Presbyter Johannes, who had routed an infidel Persian army, and would have gone to the relief of the crusaders in the Holy Land if only he had been able to find boats to ferry his army over the Tigris. In 1165 a sensational letter began to circulate around the capitals of Europe which purported to have been written by Prester John to the reigning Emperor of Byzantium.

'As Prester John', the letter boasted, 'I am lord of lords. Under heaven, I surpass in riches and virtue and power all other kings upon the whole earth.' Seventy-two kings—he claimed—were subject to him. 'Our magnificence dominates the three Indias and extends to Farther India . . . There is none to equal us in riches or in the number of our subjects. When we ride forth to war against our enemies, thirteen great and lofty crosses of gold and precious stones are carried before us in wagons, and each of them is followed by ten thousand armed foot soldiers, not counting those who have charge of baggage and provisions.'

Even in terms of military might, this was obviously an ally worth recruiting, and the wealth of Prester John was, in more ways than one, fabulous. On his behalf, giant ants, as large as small dogs, excavated gold which men loaded on to elephants, hippopotamuses and camels, 'of great stature and power', for transport to the royal treasuries. His palace was roofed with ebony; its gables were decorated with golden apples which shone resplendently by day and with carbuncles which gave forth light by night. The windows were of crystal, and the king's table was of gold and amethyst, supported on columns of ivory. 30,000 men dined every day at Prester John's expense. At table, he himself was served by 7 kings, 62 dukes, 365 counts; he sat down with 12 archbishops and 20 bishops, not to mention the patriarch of St. Thomas. In chapel he was attended by 365 abbots. 'If you ask why our sublimity assumes no higher title than the name of priest, let not your wisdom be surprised . . . We have many ministers at our court whose ecclesiastical dignity is supported by great titles and offices . . . Therefore it seems unfitting for our highness to assume such names, or to be distinguished by dignities with which our court is already full. Therefore, in our humility, we choose to be called by a lesser name and to assume a lowlier rank.'

It has been assumed that this letter was fabricated either to exalt the heretical Nestorian church or as propaganda to alarm the Saracens and thus relieve pressure on the twelfth-century crusaders. It led Pope Alexander III to assert the universal authority of the Catholic church, but the messenger he sent to Prester John disappeared. Piani de Carpine who set off to Mongolia in 1245 found no trace of Prester John in 1246, but a few years later Rubruquis (William of Rubruck) reported that this 'Nestorian shepherd' had his seat near Karakorum in Central Asia, and that he and his brother Ung had recently been defeated by Genghis Khan. Marco Polo said that Prester John was identical with the Tartar Ung Khan. But he also declared—and with justification—that Christ was the sovereign of Abyssinia, in which country three kings out of six were Christians. Europeans who read Marco Polo, and who were anxious not to lose a hero and a potential ally, now began to transfer their attention westward and to locate Prester John in the Third India—i.e. in Africa.

This trend was encouraged by the emergence of the real and hitherto unknown ruler of Ethiopia. In 1290 a commercial treaty was signed between Egypt and Genoa which so improved communications across the Mediterranean that in 1306 the Emperor of Abyssinia sent a thirty-man embassy to Europe, ostensibly to offer aid to 'the king of the Spains' in his struggle against the infidel; doubtless in return he wished for European aid in resisting the pressure of his Muslim neighbours. The cartographer, Giovanni da Carignano, interrogated the members of the mission in Genoa, and wrote a report on the government, religious observances and customs of the Abyssinians. Carignano's work has been lost, but according to a summary printed in the next century he reported 'that Prester John is set over that people as patriarch; and he says that under him are 127 archbishoprics, each of which has twenty bishops . . . It is said that their emperor is most Christian, to whom seventy-four kings and almost innumerable princes pay allegiance, except those kings who observe the laws of Muhammad but submit to the emperor in other things.'

In 1321 a traveller in India heard from Italian merchants that the way into Abyssinia, the land of Prester John, was open, and on his return he reported that this ruler waged constant war against the Muslims, and that situated close to his realm was the earthly paradise. The map of Angelino Dulcert placed Prester John in Ethiopia, and that of Abraham Cresques portrayed the upper Nile as the 'seyñoria del emperador de Ethiopia de la tera de preste iõhã', and showed churches there with flags bearing triple crosses. And Abraham Cresques's son Jafuda, who had helped prepare his father's world-map, entered the service of Henry the Navigator soon after 1420; he must have encouraged that prince's interest in Prester John now that the latter ruler was moving out of the realm of myth into something approaching reality. It was only natural that Henry should wish to explore the coasts of Africa in search, not only of the gold of Mali, but also of so wealthy and powerful a potential ally. Moreover many of the medieval world-maps already showed Africa as being surrounded by water. The voyage around it seemed feasible even before it began.

From 1422 onwards Henry began to send ships exploring southward along the coast of Morocco. Their captains viewed with repulsion the country beyond Cape Não, where the Sahara came down to the sea. There was little vegetation and no sign of human life; and without human life there could be no trade and no profit. Moreover, around Cape Bojador the shore was low and difficult to identify, while the sea was full of shoals. A league out to sea the lead showed only three fathoms of water, according to Duarte Pacheco Pereira who described the coast in 1505, and when it touched ten fathoms the land was out of sight. The winds and the currents were predominantly from the north; the difficulty was not in going south but in returning. According to Pacheco Pereira, the seamen had a punning saying: 'He who reaches Cape Não will return or não (not).' Many captains turned back before they had gone far south and on their return voyages carried out piratical attacks on Muslim

ships off the Moroccan and Granadan coasts. It has indeed
been argued that the attraction of easy gain from privateer-
ing was at least as powerful a factor as navigational difficulties
in the abandonment of these early voyages.

The main nautical difficulties were resolved because of the
greater knowledge of the wind system which came from
increased traffic to the Madeira Islands and to the Azores
after their rediscovery in 1419–20 and 1427 respectively.
From the African coast it was found to be possible to sail
towards the Azores on a reach, and then to take advantage
of variable and often favourable winds for the return
voyage to Portugal. Gil Eanes was accordingly able to
round Cape Bojador and to return in 1434. The next year
he and Baldaia passed fifty leagues beyond the cape, and in
1436 Baldaia reached a river which he assumed to be the
River of Gold of medieval maps. At the river mouth he
counted 5,000 seals. The oil and pelts derived from these
creatures were to contribute to the profit of later expeditions.

In 1437 the progress of exploration was interrupted by the
ineffectual attempt on the part of Henry and his youngest
brother, Fernando, to capture Tangier. Their troops failed
to storm the city walls, and their badly located camp was
cut off from the sea by the Moorish armies. The Portuguese
were overwhelmed in the subsequent fighting. The survivors
were granted life and liberty on the condition that Portugal
surrender Ceuta and that one of the princes remain as a
hostage until this was effected. Fernando went into a
Moorish dungeon where he stayed for the rest of his days,
for Ceuta was not given up. This disaster hastened the end of
King Duarte, who had succeeded King João I, but only
after he had foolishly decreed in his will that his Spanish-
born widow rule as regent during the minority of his eldest
son, Afonso, who was only six years of age. The clamour of

the people of Lisbon forced the Queen to withdraw in favour of Duarte's eldest surviving brother, the energetic, intelligent, cultured and much-travelled Pedro, who saw the folly of seeking territorial aggrandizement in Morocco, and instead gave new encouragement to maritime exploration and overseas trade.

At about this time maritime expeditions were facilitated by the introduction of a new type of vessel, the caravel. The caravel carried lateen sails, which had originated as an Arab rig and had reached Portugal by way of the Mediterranean. Caravels were referred to in Portugal as early as the thirteenth century, but these first prototypes were small, single-masted, and used for fishing and other off-shore sailing. By the middle of the fifteenth century they had increased in size, though they had retained their comparatively shallow draft, and now they carried two masts, later increased to three. They had the repute of being able to sail closer to the wind than the *barca* and *barinel*, two types of ship which they superseded, and they were sturdy sea-boats. It was in a vessel of this type that in 1441 Nuño Tristão sailed to within sight of Cape Branco in the north of Mauritania, and he and Gonçalves brought back captives who provided particulars about the trade of the western Sahara and who made promises of profitable ventures in the future, which were confirmed the following year when Gonçalves obtained not only slaves but also gold-dust.

There is no need to list all the expeditions which Pedro dispatched or which were financed privately and sent under Pedro's blessing. The most significant of them, under Nuño Tristão, led to the discovery in 1444 of the mouth of the Senegal, the river that marks the end of the Sahara and the beginning of the populous regions of west Africa. Dinis Dias, possibly a forebear of the more celebrated Bartolomeu

1 The Fortress of São Jorge de Mina as represented on the 'Cantino' map, c. 1502

11 Africa, from the map by Henricus Martellus Germanus, drawn in Florence c. 1489

Dias, discovered Cape Verde near the site of present-day Dakar. Later Nuno Tristão pushed onward to the mouth of the Gambia and there met his death at the hands of inhabitants who had no desire to be enslaved.

Towards the end of the 1440s, exploration was again seriously interrupted, this time by an internecine dispute among the Portuguese ruling class. The Conde de Barcelos, an illegitimate son of João I who had been elevated to the dukedom of Bragança, headed a conspiracy of noblemen, mainly rich landowners, against the regent Pedro, whose support lay mainly in the towns. Pedro's brother Henry did nothing to save him, and Pedro's daughter, who had married the young King Afonso, was powerless to influence the course of events. Pedro died with an arrow through his heart at the battle of Alfarrobeira in 1449, and, though Afonso retained the throne, the house of Bragança had started on the road to power that would lead it less than two centuries later to the Portuguese throne. Meanwhile, the land was so disorganized that it was not until 1455 that exploration could be resumed.

Once again Prince Henry assumed entire control of the operations along the African coast, which were now beginning to show a fair profit. The Venetian Cadamosto, who visited west Africa with Henry's permission, reported that from the factory or trading post of Arguin, south of Cape Branco, between 700 and 800 slaves were exported every year to Portugal, and that from every cargo Henry collected his fifth share. Cadamosto took a particular interest in malagueta 'pepper', which soon became known in Europe as 'grains of paradise', with the result that the region from which it was exported—roughly equivalent to eastern Sierra Leone and Liberia—became known as the Grain Coast. The Venetian voyager visited the mouth of the

Senegal, which—in common with many others—he believed must link up with the Niger and the Nile. There he met the Genoan Usodimare, and together their caravels sailed on to the Gambia River. Usodimare declared that from there it was a journey of only 300 leagues to the frontiers of Prester John's dominion, and that at this very time, visiting the King of Mali who was a mere six days' journey from the coast, there were five Christians from the land of Prester John.

By now, indeed, the Christian King of Abyssinia had become a less mysterious being. In 1427 two Abyssinian ambassadors had actually made their way to the court of Afonso of Aragon and proposed an alliance; the Spanish king in return dispatched thirteen craftsmen to Ethiopia (all of whom died on the way) and even considered offering the hand of his daughter in marriage to the Negus. In 1441, two Ethiopian delegates from Jerusalem attended the Council of Florence, and at last, in 1452, an Abyssinian ambassador arrived in Lisbon. Prince Henry must have been greatly encouraged to hear from Usodimare that Prester John's empire extended so far westward, and in 1456 he readily gave Usodimare and Cadamosto permission to continue their explorations. They reached a Rio Grande, which was probably the Geba, and admired the Bijagos Islands off the coast of Guinea. Later Henry sent out Pedro de Sintra, who explored as far as a Serra Leoa, which we now call Sierra Leone; this was the limit of European exploration along the coasts of Africa by the time Henry died in 1460.

The influence of Prince Henry on exploration has often been exaggerated. Of the thirty-five known voyages and expeditions from Portugal between 1419 and 1460 which have been listed by the historian Magalhães Godinho, only eight were actually initiated by Henry and for two others he was partly responsible. The most energetic period was in fact during the regency of Pedro, when Henry was inactive; in this period 200 leagues of the 360 leagues of African coastline charted by 1460 were discovered, an achievement which is remarkable when one considers that during most of this period the captains and pilots of the Portuguese ships had little to assist them but rhumb-lined charts, compasses and their love of the sea. With such simple means they often performed extraordinary feats of seamanship. The survivors of the fatal Tristão expedition numbered only seven, of whom two were grievously wounded, yet they managed to navigate almost back to Portugal, without sighting land for two months, before they were succoured by a corsair.

The first record of celestial observations was in fact as late as 1451, when a sister of Afonso V travelled to Italy on a vessel which carried 'skilled astronomers, well versed in the stars and the ways of the poles'. Cadamosto referred to the height of the pole star, not in degrees, but as the height of a third of a lance above the horizon. Diogo Gomes wrote of his voyage to Guinea in 1460: 'I had a quadrant when I went to these parts, and I wrote the height of the arctic pole on the board of the quadrant.' In her delightful book, *The Haven-finding Art*, Professor E. G. R. Taylor quotes this statement as proof that charts were not yet marked in latitudes, nor were the quadrants marked in degrees; the pilots of the day simply noted on their quadrants at each locality where the plumb-line crossed the board.

Shortly after Prince Henry's death, Diogo Gomes sailed in 1461 to extend exploration of the African coastline to a point a few miles beyond Cape Mesurado, in present-day Liberia, but for some years this was the end of state-inspired voyages of discovery. The resources of the royal treasury were consumed by the repeated adventures in Morocco on which King Afonso embarked after he came of age and took over the government of Portugal.

By now, in any case, the trade on the coast of Guinea was flourishing, because the Portuguese had learnt the long-term advantages of peaceful intercourse over kidnappings and violence. This made voyages to Africa attractive to speculative traders, and, since no member of the royal house now retained an active interest in exploration, Afonso leased the Guinea trade in 1468 to one Fernão Gomes, 'an honourable citizen of Lisbon', for the sum of 200 milreis a year, on condition that each year he explore one hundred leagues of coastline, beginning at Serra Leoa. In spite of the voyage of Diogo Gomes, traders were not yet familiar with the coast between Serra Leoa and Cape Mesurado. The lease to Fernão Gomes explicitly excluded trade on the African mainland facing the Cape Verde Islands, which had been granted to settlers on the islands, and also the trade of the factory-fortress of Arguin, which had been granted to Prince João, Afonso's young son; the latter Gomes eventually leased for an extra 100 milreis a year. One condition of his lease was that he sell ivory at a fixed price to the King, while he was allowed to acquire only one civet-cat a year (which was regarded as a great concession); otherwise he enjoyed a monopoly of the African trade.

Except for a few lines in the sixteenth-century chronicle of João de Barros, almost nothing is known about the discoveries which was financed by Fernão Gomes. By 1471 João de Santarem and Pero Escolar had voyaged as far as Shama, in present-day Ghana; they traded there for gold and sailed on to the Aldeia da Duas Partes—a village in two sections an arrow's flight apart—which proved to be so remunerative for the trade in gold that it received the name of Mina—the Mine. Shortly afterwards Fernão do Po discovered an island in the Bight of Biafra which he named Formosa, but which afterwards was to be known by an adaptation of his own name—Fernando Po. Other islands in the Bight were discovered by unknown navigators. One was São Tomé, and another, originally called Santo Antonio, was later renamed Principe in honour of Prince João. The last important voyage under the lease granted to Fernão Gomes, which finally expired after a year's extension in 1477, was that in which Rui de Sequeira explored south of the Bight of Biafra as far as Cape Santa Catarina, 1° 53′ south of the equator and now in the country of Gabon. The contract under which these discoveries were made brought wealth and ennoblement to Gomes and prosperity to Portugal. It also notably prepared the way for the explorations of Cão and Dias.

Already, in 1474, King Afonso had charged Prince João, now nineteen years old, with the administration of the trade with Guinea. At João's instigation, Afonso published it abroad that the Popes had granted the Portuguese crown the lands and seas of Guinea southward from Cape Não (though the grant was not in fact made official until Pope Alexander VI in 1493 issued his celebrated bull dividing the world's unknown lands between Portugal and Spain), and that no person—under pain of excommunication and severe civil penalties—might go to those parts to trade or to make war.

On Afonso's death in 1481, his son ascended the throne as João II. One of his first acts was to order the construction of a fortified trading post on the Mina coast, and in January 1482 a squadron under Diogo de Azambuja anchored off the Aldeia das Duas Partes. In the dank equatorial heat, the Portuguese landed in their rich and colourful garments of brocade and silk, and assured the local ruler, whose scanty garb of gold chains round his neck and gold beads in his hair excited the visitors' cupidity, that their King wished to trade with him, and that in order to protect the rich trade goods that would be imported it was necessary to build a warehouse and fort. Such a building on his territory would undoubtedly contribute to the African ruler's increased importance.

In reply, that monarch appears to have commented in a somewhat forthright manner on the behaviour of the Europeans he had so far met, but the Portuguese expedition was so powerful that he was in no position to reject its demands; aboard his dozen vessels Azambuja carried a force of no less than 600 armed men. Of these no less than a hundred were stonemasons and carpenters, and out of the ships' holds was brought stone already dressed in Portugal for the doorways and window recesses, together with lime, timber and tiles. Quarrymen broke and shaped stone for the walls from a rocky outcrop on a small peninsula that gave shelter to the anchorage, and on the platform which they cleared in this way arose the massive fortress of São Jorge de Mina. São Jorge de Mina provided a strong and convenient base where Cão, and later Dias, could refit and resupply their vessels and refresh their crews, in preparation for their historic explorations to the south.

II

The First Voyage of Diogo Cão

IT was in the same year as work commenced on the massive walls of São Jorge de Mina that Diogo Cão set out on the first of the succession of voyages that led, in a few years, to the Portuguese rounding of Africa and the discovery of the route to India and eventually to the Far East.

Almost nothing is known of the origins or the early life of Diogo Cão. It has been generally assumed that he was descended from a family of the name of Cão which lived during the later Middle Ages in the province of Tras-os-Montes, in the extreme north of Portugal, near the site of the present-day town of Vila Real. Diogo's grandfather distinguished himself in the wars against the Castilians which preserved the freedom of Portugal at the end of the fourteenth century, and his father served King Afonso V. Diogo himself must have been born about the middle of the fifteenth century, though there are no records which suggest the exact date. He was certainly reared in a tradition that demanded military service on both land and sea. Such service, by the time Diogo attained manhood, extended to the coast of Guinea where the Portuguese were seeking to impose, as they later did in the Indian Ocean and the Indonesian archipelago, a *mare clausum*, a sea forbidden to outsiders.

It is only in 1480 that Diogo Cão first enters history as an identifiable personage, and then in a rather uncomplimentary fashion. In 1479 a certain Eustace de la Fosse, a

2. West African coastline, Cape Santa Catarina to Cape Cross

native of Flanders, travelled with trade goods from Bruges to Seville, and then, in the company of a number of Spanish vessels, sailed on an interloping voyage to the coast of Guinea. Early on the morning of the 6th January 1480 as he lay at anchor off the Aldeia das Duas Partes, a number of Portuguese vessels suddenly emerged from a bank of fog and opened fire on him. He was forced to surrender; the Castilian vessels had been captured the previous day, and all the interlopers were ransacked by the Portuguese. One of the ships was then handed over to the main body of the prisoners, who were given one sail and one anchor, with minimal supplies of biscuit and water, and set free with permission to get home to Spain if they could.

The senior officers were retained for interrogation in Portugal by Prince João. At first de la Fosse was placed on a vessel commanded by a captain he called Fernand de les Vaux—undoubtedly Fernão do Po. De la Fosse was treated considerately, but the ship was travelling 200 leagues beyond Mina before it returned to Portugal, and the prisoner protested vociferously against the unnecessary journey. He was accordingly transferred to the caravel of Diogo Cão, whom he described simply as 'un fourbe' (a knave). With his share of the prize money from capturing the interlopers, Cão had bought de la Fosse's ship, and, to add insult to injury, he forced him to barter his own trade-goods along the coast for the benefit of his Portuguese captors; at the end of each day de la Fosse was put to the humiliating and infuriating procedure of giving Cão an exact account of the day's transactions.

It may well have been Cão's behaviour during this encounter with Flemish and Castilian interlopers that brought him to the attention of Prince João, and caused the latter, soon after his own accession to the Portuguese throne, to appoint Cão to the command of what was evidently conceived as an important venture of exploration. No trace has actually survived of the *regimento* or instruction which the King issued to Cão, but the sixteenth-century chronicler, Fernão Lopes de Castanheda, one of the most reliable recorders of the period, leaves little doubt of the magnitude of the scheme within which Cão's voyage fitted in the King's vision. 'João II,' Castanheda remarked, 'being of very high thoughts and desirous of enlarging his dominions and ennobling them in the service of our Lord, determined to continue the discovery of the coast of Guinea which his predecessor had commenced. Along that coast, it seemed to him, he would be able to discover the dominions of Prester John of the Indies of whom he had had report; so that by that way it would be possible to enter India and he would be able to send his captains to fetch those riches which the Venetians brought for sale.'

From this it seems clear that, apart from the basic task of exploring and charting the coast of Africa beyond Gabon, and searching out the sources of possible trade, Cão was instructed to look out for a route to the Christian empire of Abyssinia, while the possibility was not ruled out of rounding an Africa which contemporary maps, such as those of Andrea Bianco and Fra Mauro, already indicated as surrounded by water. Sixteen years before Vasco da Gama actually reached the Malabar coast of India, it is evident that the King of Portugal and his advisers were already seeking a means to tap by sea the rich spice trade from the Indies which the Venetians were then monopolizing through their friendly relations with the Muslim leaders of the Levant who controlled the routes through the Red Sea and by land through the deserts of Mesopotamia and Arabia.

By this time the activities of the Portuguese along the

African coast had become—in spite of official attempts to maintain a close secrecy—the object of growing interest in other parts of Europe, as the interloping efforts of de la Fosse and his companions had shown. The interest was particularly strong among the bankers of the Rhineland cities who were impressed by the increasing flow of gold into European markets, and among the map-makers of Italy, still one of the great maritime nations of Europe and the birth-place of notable explorers like Columbus, Verazzano and John Cabot. Map-makers in Florence, and also in Spain and Germany, gained rapid knowledge of the discoveries of both Cão and his successor Dias, and incorporated them in charts, some of them made as early as 1489, which have survived in various European libraries and museums. The methods employed to gain such information are illustrated by the history of the anonymous planisphere known as the 'Cantino Chart' which is preserved in the Estense Library of Modena. Alberto Cantino's claim to be named in this connection is somewhat spurious, since he did not draw the map himself. As secret agent of Ercole d'Este, then Duke of Ferrara, Cantino went to Portugal disguised as a horse dealer, and for twelve gold ducats he bribed a Portuguese cartographer to copy the official map of the known world as recent explorations had revealed it. Cantino sent the map to Duke Ercole in November 1502, and later, as other spies provided further information, additions were made to it. On this map are marked no less than 109 place-names from Cape Santa Catarina in Gabon to the farthest point reached by Dias beyond the Cape of Good Hope.

If the Italians used every means to obtain exact information about the Portuguese discoveries, the Germans were not above claiming spurious credit for their own compatriots, and one of the most interesting reports of the time appears in the Nürnberg Chronicle of 1493. It records that in 1483 King João of Portugal sent out an expedition consisting of two vessels, one of them commanded by Canus (i.e. Cão), 'a Portuguese, and Martinus Bohemus, a German, a native of Nürnberg in upper Germany, of good family, who had a thorough knowledge of the countries of the world and was most patient of the sea and who had gained, by many years, navigation, a thorough knowledge beyond Ptolemy's longitudes to the west. These two, by favour of the gods, sailed, not far from the coast, to the south, and having crossed the equinoctial line entered another world where looking to the east their shadow fell southwards, to the right. They had thus by their diligence discovered another world not known to us, and for many years searched for in vain by the Genoese. Having thus pursued their voyage they came back after twenty-six months to Portugal, many having died owing to the heat.'

Martinus Bohemus was the German geographer Martin Behaim, whose celebrated globe, which he constructed between 1490 and 1493, has been a matter of controversy to scholars of Magellan as well as of Cão. The claims for Behaim's connection with Cão's voyage can be dismissed as mere self-advertisement, for there is no evidence to support them and many reasons to dismiss them. There is no likelihood that the suspicious Portuguese would have given a foreigner joint command of so important an expedition, while Behaim's globe is in fact less accurate so far as Africa south of Guinea is concerned than some other contemporary maps. It is possible that the German did indeed travel as far as Guinea, and he may indeed on some occasion have been on the same ship as Cão, but that is as much as one is justified in assuming.

44

Other cartographers, on the other hand, recorded information relating to the discoveries of Cão, and later of Dias, which is invaluable in the absence of the original logs or journals of the voyages, and the royal instructions to their commanders, all of which must have perished when the papers of the House of Guinea and India, which governed Portuguese trading and colonization in newly discovered territories, were destroyed in the Lisbon earthquake of 1755 and the great fire that swept the city in its wake. Among the most important of these near-contemporary maps and charts are the 'Ginea Portugalexe', a Venetian copy in the British Museum of a lost Portuguese original; the world-map drawn by Henricus Martellus Germanus in Florence and contained in his *Insularium Illustratum*, compiled about 1489 and also in the British Museum; the world-map drawn by Juan de la Cosa for the Spanish authorities in 1500 and now preserved in the Museo Naval in Madrid; and the already-mentioned map, copied from a Portuguese original, which Alberto Cantino obtained for the Duke of Ferrara. In the absence of first-hand accounts of the voyages, the names of places shown on these maps compiled a few years after the discoveries of Cão and Dias are invaluable as indications of the routes which the explorers followed, but they remain second-hand evidence, and it is for this reason that the discovery of the actual *padrões* or stone columns erected by Cão and Dias was so important, since these would provide the only completely reliable confirmation of the extent of their discoveries.

There are not even any reliable surviving records of the number of ships or men that Cão took on his first voyage, but here we can probably accept the assertion of the Nürnberg Chronicle that he sailed with two ships, since this would have been the minimum for such an expedition, and the two *padrões* Cão erected were probably carried, one in each ship, as ballast. Doubtless he was accompanied by the best pilots and sailing masters available, but the name of only one of his officers is known—Pero Dias, the brother of the great Bartolomeu—and that only because Cão named after him a cape on the coast of Gabon, a circumstance which leads one to speculate that Pero may have been his lieutenant. It seems equally certain that Cão was issued with the latest aids to navigation. Azambuja took an astrolabe with him on his voyage to establish the fort at Mina, and it is unlikely that Cão was less well equipped; while the oldest known Portuguese nautical almanac was calculated for the year 1483, and it has been suggested by the naval and cartographic historian, Commander Teixeira da Mota, that this was actually produced for Cão's first voyage, and that thereafter Portuguese pilots calculated latitudes as a matter of course. This alone would make Cão's first voyage a landmark in the history of navigation.

Cão sailed from Portugal in 1482, certainly before the end of August, as we shall see in discussing the inscription on one of the *padrões* he erected on the coast of Angola, and probably in the spring. It has been suggested that he left Portugal with Azambuja's squadron, bound for Mina, but it seems more likely that he departed afterwards so that he and his men would not only be spared participation in the heavy labour of establishing the factory there, but would also be able to take advantage of its presence when he anchored in the sheltered bay to the east of the partly completed fortress of São Jorge, where his men could rest awhile, make such repairs to their caravels as had become necessary during the voyage from Portugal, and replenish their supplies of fresh water, provisions and firewood.

From Cape Santa Catarina, the virtual limit at this time

of Portuguese exploration, Cão's instructions—which related to the discovery of new trading possibilities as much as of new lands—doubtless required him to follow the coast as closely as possible, though he could not sail too near in, for the waters here are so shallow that even a mile and a half off the Cape the lead reaches only seven and a half fathoms.

Southward from Cape Santa Catarina the coast was monotonous, with a low ridge facing on to the sea, cut by small rivers, and masking an inland complex of lagoons and marshes. The first landmark of any importance was one whose naming illustrated the crusading spirit which was one of the motives of Portuguese exploration; christened by Cão the Serra do Espirito Santo—the range of the Holy Spirit—it consisted of two lofty table-topped hills, divided by a valley, rising behind a range of lower hills separated by a belt of lofty rain forest from the coastal mangrove swamps. Beyond the Serra do Espirito Santo (still called on modern charts the Espirito Santo Hills) Cão came to the cape he named for Pero Dias, though now it is uncertain which of several rather undistinguished headlands in the locality he chose to honour his fellow navigator. He sailed on to the mouth of the Nyanga River, near the site of the present town of Setté Cama, and there, impressed by the broadness of the beaches, he named one of them the Praia Imperatoris—the Beach of the Emperor.

South from the Nyanga, Cão sailed within sight of broad, sandy beaches, with marshy mangrove swamps and areas of pandanus scrub behind them until he came to Cape Mayoumba, otherwise known as Panga Point, a well-known mark for seamen which the American *Sailing Directions for the Southwest Coast of Africa* describe as—seen from the north— 'three or four saddle-shaped summits. On the seaward side is a deep red cliff surmounted by dense woods, forming one of the most conspicuous objects of the coast.' The prominence of the red cliff leaves no doubt that this is the Ponta das Barreiras (Cape of the Cliffs) which appears on the Spanish map of Juan da Cosa, and that Cão gave it this name.

Rounding this spectacular promontory, Cão sailed into the broad and beautifully regular arc of Mayoumba Bay, with its sandy beaches and the background of wooded hills through which the Mayoumba River breaks its way. This bay is the southern limit of the equatorial rain belt, and south of it Cão sailed along an increasingly sandy shore, behind whose dunes the vegetation became steadily less luxuriant. Here and there the features of the landscape attracted his attention, and found their eventual places on the maps that were based on his voyages. Banda Point, for example, appears on the map that was obtained for the Duke of Ferrara as the Ponta das Montes (Mountain Point), and the two lofty and striking hills now known as the Mamelles—or Paps—of Banda are shown as Dous Montes (the Two Hills).

Sailing now along the coast of modern Zaire, past mangrove swamps and groves of wild palms, with monotonous ridges forming the backdrop to his view of the land, Cão reached the mouth of the Kouilou River, overlooked by small wooded hills, and shortly afterwards sailed into the deep waters of Loango Bay, perhaps the most spectacularly handsome feature of the coastscape that he had yet viewed. He called it the Beautiful Bay, and thus it appears on the early maps as Praia Formosa. The bay is three miles across, with a narrow beach and behind it a thick line of dark green trees. The headland to the north (now called Pointe Indienne) rises to bare and deeply furrowed reddish hills which culminate in cliffs, and other cliffs extend behind the bay itself. At the head of the bay there is a brackish lagoon

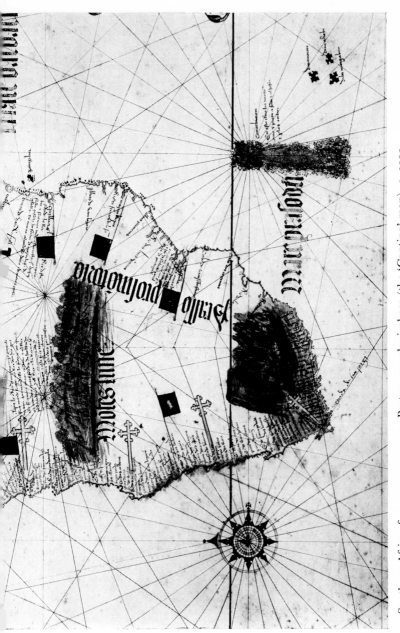

III Southern Africa, from an anonymous Portuguese planisphere (the 'Cantino' map), c. 1502

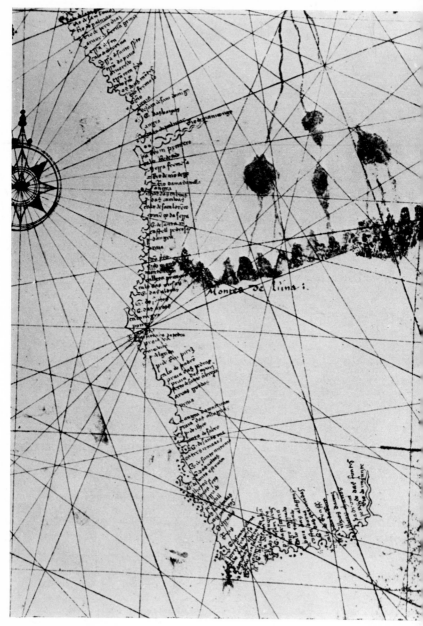

IV Southern Africa, from an anonymous Portuguese map (known as the Kunstmann III), c. 1506. The lines are rhumbs drawn through arbitrarily selected points to indicate compass bearings

into which several springs discharge fresh water, and to the south stretch hills which merge eventually into a wooded range that on one of the contemporary maps bears the name Sera da Praia Fermosa de S. Domenego. If this name was indeed conferred by Cão, as seems certain, it suggests that he sailed down this part of the coast on the day of Saint Dominic, which is 24th May; the year, by now, would be 1483.

Cão sailed on, past Landana Bay and the spectacular line of red cliffs beneath which Molemba Bay lies in semi-concealment, for it is one of those rather typical Central African bays which penetrate to the south-east and are protected by spits of sand produced by the current that flows from the south and by the prevalent south-westerly swell. 'Coming from seaward,' remarks that exhaustive guide for navigators, the *Africa Pilot*, 'these shallow bays are very difficult of recognition, as the low points, not being distinctive in character, are absorbed in the background, and this is especially the case in the appearance of Bahia de Molemba when viewed from the offing.' But there is no mistaking the spectacular background, and the Ponta da Barreira Vermelho (Point of the Vermilion Cliff) which appears on more than one of the late fifteenth-century maps is undoubtedly Molemba Point, a grass-covered tongue of land that projects from the base of these cliffs. If Cão probably missed Molemba Bay, he could not have failed to observe and be impressed by Cabinda Bay, where valleys buried in luxuriant verdure flowed down towards the shore between green hills and tall cliffs. It was a shallow bay— the three-fathom line here runs a mile and a half out from the shore—and Cão cannot have sailed close inshore. Instead, the people came out in their own small craft to visit his ship, for this is the Golfo das Almadias, the Bay of

Dugout Canoes, as it appears on the early maps, and Cão gave the name Ponta das Almadias to the cape which we now call Cabinda Point.

It may well be that this was the first place in which Cão was able to carry on any trading, for it is significant that no mention at all of the earlier part of his voyage, as far as the mouth of the Congo, appears among the fragmentary mentions of his discoveries that occur in the sixteenth-century Portuguese chronicles, and the reason for this may well be contained in a remark made by Pacheco Pereira, who was at Mina with Azambuja when Cão sailed south from that fort. 'In the portion which fell to the most serene Dom João to discover, from Cape Santa Catarina onwards,' Pacheco declares in the introduction to his *Esmeraldo de Situ Orbis* (a rutter compiled between 1505 and 1508), 'most of the country is largely desert, and in the small part that is inhabited little or no commerce is to be found; had it been rich in trade like the region I have previously described I should have had more pleasure in describing the profit we could have received from that region.'

The implication is clear: to the commercially minded Portuguese the only parts of Cão's voyage that held much interest were those that led to trade. And this seems to have been the effect of his encounter with the people who came out to him in their canoes at Cabinda Bay, for afterwards the Portuguese established themselves there, and to this day Cabinda remains an enclave of their colony of Angola, pinched between the sea and the two independent Congolese republics.

From Cabinda to the mouth of the Congo Cão sailed beside a low coastline, luxuriant and green, from which the sea-bed sloped very gradually, so that the off-shore waters remained extremely shallow; inland rose reddish hills that continued to the mouth of the Congo. At last Cão's ship, rounded the point which he called the Cabo das Palmas covered to this day with palm trees and terminating in a rufous-coloured hillock which led later seamen to give it the more colourful name of Red Devil's Point (Ponta do Diablo Vermelho). Situated at latitude 5° 44', this low cape marked the beginning of the estuary of the great river.

It is only at this stage on his voyage that the sixteenth-century chroniclers begin to pay attention to Cão's activities, and his achievements emerge for a brief while into recorded action. Barros portrays him sailing into the mangrove-lined mouth of the Congo (which one of the maps that depended on Cão's discoveries named so appropriately the Rio Poderoso—powerful river) where anchoring to the leeward of a small point, he raised his first *padrão*, and dedicated it to St. George, who was the patron saint of Portugal as well as of England. The point was named, on the early maps, the Cabo do Padrão. According to Pacheco Pereira, it carried three inscriptions, in Latin, in Portuguese and in Arabic. Barros mentions only Latin and Portuguese, but this was one of the *padrões* which did not survive, and one is thrown into doubt by the fact that the other *padrão* of Cão's first voyage, which was preserved, carried an inscription only in Portuguese. It is not impossible, however, that Pacheco Pereira, who was so nearly contemporary with Cão, may have been right, and that an Arabic inscription was included on this particular cross because it would be planted in a place thought to be close to the domains of Prester John.

Cão's first *padrão* did not stand long on its little headland. Already, in 1645, when the Capuchin missionaries arrived on their way to the kingdom of Congo, they saw a large stone lying on the beach, and the local inhabitants told them that it was a fragment of Cão's cross, which the Dutch had broken as a monument of the Catholic Portuguese King when they invaded Angola in 1641. Forty years later, in 1682, Friar Merolla saw some fragments of the landmark bearing the royal coat of arms and an inscription which, unfortunately, he did not record. A later tradition that the *padrão* was destroyed through being made a target for shelling by an English naval ship is thus certainly untrue.

In fact, parts of the monument did survive in a manner certainly not anticipated by either Cão or his royal and Catholic master. In the 1880s the Portuguese representative stationed at the mouth of the Congo, F. J. de França, searched for the missing *padrão* and was unsuccessful because later charts mistakenly indicated the Ponta da Moita Seca, the westernmost projection south of the mouth of the Congo, as the Cabo de Padrão. Baron Schwerin, Professor of Geography at Lund University, who had examined the sites of other Cão *padrões*, encouraged França to search more widely, and eventually the latter heard of the existence in the locality of a fetish much revered by the local inhabitants and made of stone. Since there is no natural stone in the locality, França's interest was immediately aroused. It was obvious that the stone had been there for many generations, since one informant told França that it had fallen from the skies in the lifetime of his great-great-grandfather. For a long time the tribesmen refused to reveal the whereabouts of their fetish, but eventually França persuaded the chief to hold a palaver, and after assurances that the appropriate deity would be placated, the site was revealed. The fragments were covered in cloth wrappings, and when these were removed França and Schwerin had no hesitation in identifying them as parts of the *padrão*. The next day the Portuguese gunboat *Massabi* dropped anchor off the site;

the captain landed, examined the remains, and hurried back to fire a salute in honour of Diogo Cão.

Among the other Europeans whom França invited to view the fragments was a British commercial agent stationed at Banana, close to the mouth of the Congo. His name was R. E. Dennett, and, after making his examination, he wrote a report which has a special interest because it vividly suggests the appearance of the site where, on that summer day of 1483, Cão went ashore to raise his first monument. Dennett described how he landed on the peninsula, and walked past a submerged cemetery and past a grove of palm trees some of them half-submerged and others on the beach with the waters dashing around their roots, suggesting that over the years the level of the land had changed.

'We now struck inland, walking across a low-lying plain, once, I have no doubt, under water, but now covered with grass, vetches with their pretty yellow flowers, and the grasping "mpema" or seaside bean; there a graceful acacia and there a mteva or fan palm tree. Five minutes' walk brought us to higher ground, which towards the interior was thickly overgrown with mangrove trees, while facing the beach the mteva palms were almost smothered in thick shrubs and undergrowth common to the country . . . We had now only to wind our way through the bush for a short distance when we caught sight of the venerated stone nestled in the centre of a little grove and cleared of all its sacred cloth . . . I found the base of the original column resting on a portion of the column itself that had broken off far above the base, judging from its dimensions. Two round stones lay on the ground close to the foot of the base. The base measured about 68 centimetres, was well squared, tapered to the lower extremity and rounded where the pillar had been broken.

The rounded part of the pillar upon which the base rested measured about 18 inches in length, and about 12 inches in diameter; the two ball-shaped pieces about 7 inches and 9 inches in diameter respectively. All the parts are cut out of white marble. I breakfasted with Sen. França, who is full of the discovery and hopes to complete the discovery by unearthing other pieces and perhaps some relics of Diogo Cão.'

But this was not done, perhaps because the tribesmen did not wish their fetish to be further disturbed, and only the miserable stump of the column, made of Portuguese limestone and not of the marble Dennett described, reached Portugal and eventually found a place in the museum of the Sociedade de Geografia de Lisboa. The rest doubtless remained, the object of a worship the pious Cão would undoubtedly have abhorred.

While Cão's caravels lay at anchor just within the Congo estuary, they were surrounded by dugout canoes filled with curious countrymen, and when the seamen hoisted their heavy burden ashore and carried it laboriously across the spit of land to the Atlantic shore, the Africans flocked inquisitively about them. Cão's interpreters attempted to converse with them, but could not understand the language, though they did gather that the river itself was called the Zaire, that it ran through a mighty kingdom called Congo, and that the king of this realm lived a considerable way off in the interior.

Gathering the impression of a well-ordered society, Cão took the risk of asking the local tribesmen to guide to their king a small delegation of Portuguese. He proposed to await their return at an agreed time. After double that time had passed, and his men had still not come back, Cão kidnapped four of the inhabitants of a local village and held them as hostages against the return of his men; he also hoped to gain from studying his captives some knowledge of their language and their customs. He explained by signs to the rest of the tribesmen that after fifteen moons had passed he would come back and return the hostages, provided he found the Portuguese awaiting him, alive and well.

The account by Barros ceases at this point, and he does not report Cão's voyage southward from the Congo. We can assume, however, that Cão waited as long as he could for his men before he sailed on, and it is even possible that he did not take the hostages until he returned on his homeward voyage and still found no trace of the men who journeyed towards the capital of Congo and who fate was then unknown. It is also likely that, before he set out southward, he sailed at least some distance up the estuary of the Congo to establish that it was indeed a river and not a channel leading, as Fra Mauro's map suggested, to the Indian Ocean; Barros, indeed, hints at such a reconnaissance.

Sailing out of the mouth of the Congo, Cão and his ships passed and saluted the *padrão* as a symbol of Portuguese dominion, and ran down the coast which now trended south-east by south. On this coast the weather is rarely anything but fine, but both the south and south-westerly winds that prevail at all seasons and the north-setting current must have delayed the progress of the expedition. Many tacks off shore must have been necessary, though Cão doubtless took advantage of the nightly land breezes. Soon the regular red cliffs that line the coast south of the Congo gave way to a more broken shore, with rocky points alternating with sandy coves, while in the hinterland wooded hillsides broken by parkland could be seen. It was —and is to this day—a most attractive coastline. It is not entirely easy to identify the names given on the early maps with the natural features which we know exist along this coast, but it can probably be assumed that the rivers which were called the Fernão Vaz, the Mondego and the Madalena correspond to those which we now know as the M'brige, the Loge and the Dande. The naming of the Madalena is germane to the chronology of the voyage, since it suggests that the river was sighted and named on the day of Mary Magdalen, which is celebrated on the 22nd July.

It seems likely that Cão spent some time in the large and perfectly sheltered harbour of Luanda. The Portuguese recognized the value of the site, where in the early seventeenth century they raised the fortress of São Miguel, and later created the capital of Angola, and it is likely that Cão devoted some attention to the site as a potential base for trading. Certainly, he established contact with the inhabitants of the Isles of Goats, as he called them, which shield the harbour. These people enjoyed a certain prosperity not only because the fishing was excellent, but also because they gathered small shells about the size of a pine-kernel, which they called *zinbos*, and which served as currency in the kingdom of Congo, where, according to Pacheco Pereira, fifty bought a fowl and three hundred a goat, while favours or rewards granted by the sovereign were paid in such shells 'in the same way as our princes bestow money . . . on those who deserve it and often on those who do not'. The shells, as Magellan's chronicler Pigafetta learned later in the sixteenth century, were gathered by women who dived into the water to a depth of two yards and more, and filled their baskets with sand out of which they sifted the shells. Such shells were found quite widely along the coast, but those of Luanda were most valued, 'being transparent, and in colours somewhat like the chrysolite . . .' They were valued, in that kingdom, more highly than either silver or gold.

Sailing southward from Luanda along the Angolan coast, Cão was forced out to sea by the shallowness of the waters—for even seven miles from the coast the depth is often a mere ten fathoms—and this need to keep a safe offing doubtless explains why he failed to notice, on both his southward and his homeward voyages, the mouth of the Cuanza, the second largest river in Angola. Had he sailed there in the rainy season he could not have failed to observe it, for then the silt suspended in its waters discolours the ocean for ten or even, in some years, fifteen miles off shore.

South of Luanda it is again difficult to identify all the features shown on the old maps as one follows the coastline where red and white cliffs, often topped by verdant bush, alternate until the land falls to the broad plain that faces the sea at Benguela. But one place leaps into sudden relief because in his rutter, Pacheco Pereira links it with Cão in a very specific way. He refers to a Ponta das Canboas—a Point of the Fish-weirs, which he places at $10\frac{1}{2}°$ south, about twenty leagues below Luanda. The name was given, said Pacheco, 'because when Diogo Cão, *cavaleiro*, servant of King João (may he rest with god) discovered this land, he found there some fish-weirs in which the negroes were fishing, and because of this he gave it the same name'. The point, Pacheco continued, was fringed with rocks, while beyond the cape was a very small river which was hardly more than a tidal creek; 'and here there is no trade and nothing worthy of being written about.' It was the lack of other trade, of course, that turned the Portuguese on this coast into slavers and made the history of Angola so tragic for so many generations.

Yet even this place, so visually evoked by the chronicler, is hard to identify, and scholars have advanced the rival claims of different headlands, though it seems that the

Cabo das Tres Pontas, in latitude 10° 20′ south, accords most closely with Pacheco's description.

South from the Cabo das Tres Pontas, the Ponta de São Lourenço, which is probably to be identified with the remarkable headland known as the Morro de Benguela, on the southern side of the Bay of Benguela, suggests another date, for the feast of that saint falls on the 10th August. In this locality also appears a Rio de Paul, with a Villa Grossa (a large town) upon its banks, and this is almost certainly the Catumbela River, whose fertile valley, now supporting a luxuriant growth of sugar cane, would have supported even in those days a denser population than the coastline which Cão had been following. South of the Rio de Paul, the early maps mark an Angra de Santa Maria, which has not been clearly identified. The name probably refers to the day of the Assumption of Our Lady and suggests that Cão sailed along this part of the coast on the 15th August. It is curious that he does not mention the inlet that became the excellent modern harbour of Lobito; doubtless it was masked from his view as he sailed at a safe offing by the long, low sandspit that protects it from the sea.

Cão was now nearing the end of his voyage as he sailed south of Benguela, past the spectacular cone-shaped hill of the Ponta do Sombreiro, crowned by a cliff-faced circular table, and past the rising ground that extends beyond the Bay of Elephants to the bold promontory of Cape Choca, whose cliffs descend to the sea. Cão named this fortress-like rock the Cape of Alter Pedroso, after the castle of the same name that lies in the marches of Evora in Portugal. Alter Pedroso, founded after this land was reconquered from the Moors, became an apanage of the military order of São Bento de Aviz in the fourteenth century; as Diogo de Azambuja, the builder and commander of Mina, was not

only a cavalier of that order but also *comendador* of Alter
Pedroso in Portugal, there is no reason to doubt that Cão
named the headland after him.

Beyond this cape the land rose to a range of granite hills
that fall in cliffs to the sea; the rock is studded with mica
and quartz, and, as the *Africa Pilot* remarks, 'one of the
cliffs, abounding in the former, reflects the sun's rays to a
considerable distance, like a vast mirror.' The hills project
into a headland that falls jaggedly to the sea, and the rocks
at its base when Cão sighted it were alive with a heaving
brown mass of seals, whose barks and cries must have
reminded him of the shouts of the crowd at a bullfight. He
was so impressed by them that he called the place Cabo do
Lobo (Seal Cape). There are small bays sheltered by islands
on each side of the Cabo do Lobo (which later became
known as the Cabo de Santa Maria), and Cão may have
landed either in the Baía dos Pássaros (the Bay of the Birds)
to the north or the smaller bay, sheltered by the Ilhéu do
Pina (Pine Island) to the south. A small river that would
have provided fresh water flows into the latter bay. It was
at this point that Cão decided to erect his second *padrão*,
and the reason for that decision was doubtless that at this
point he turned back, for the maps which were based on
his voyage now become inaccurate and the coastlines they
portray fade into the unknown. Why he turned back is not
recorded. He can hardly have imagined that he had reached
the southern limit of Africa. To unload the heavy *padrão*,
and to carry it up the nose of the point on to the rocky
platform where it remained until the late nineteenth century
was a heavy and laborious task, and could hardly have
been performed by a crew suffering severely from that
scourge of early navigators, scurvy. The most likely explana-
tion, then, appears to be that Cão was aware of running

out of provisions on a coast where they could not easily be renewed.

The *padrão* was dedicated to St. Augustine, so that it must have been erected on the 28th August 1483, and Cão must have made up his mind to return round about that time. He had explored an unknown coastline that extended southward through twelve degrees of latitude, a total of 700 miles, or probably a great deal more if one takes into account the fact that Cão cannot possibly have sailed in anything near a straight line, owing to the difficulties created by the prevalent winds.

The *padrão* remained where the explorer had placed it for more than four centuries, undisturbed by hostile invaders or African animists in search of fetishes. It was eventually removed in 1892 and shipped back to Lisbon, where it was housed in the museum of the Sociedade de Geografia and became the first important relic of the early Portuguese explorers of Africa to be available to scholars. It consisted of a column 1·69 metres high, surmounted by a square block 0·47 metres high, with a cross standing above it. On one side of the block was a coat of arms, while an inscription covered the other three sides—an inscription, as we have said, in Portuguese only. It was the deciphering of this inscription, and the critical examination of the coat of arms by the Portuguese historian Luciano Cordeiro, which finally established that Cão had in fact sailed about two years before the date which the sixteenth-century Portuguese chroniclers attributed to him. That such an error should have arisen so shortly after the voyage is hard to believe and impossible to explain, but the evidence brought forward by Cordeiro is unanswerable. Cão cannot have sailed in any year but 1482.

Cordeiro began by recognizing that the coat of arms was

in the medieval style, which had been introduced by King João I (1385–1433) and which has been described heraldically as 'five escutcheons in cross azure, each charged with as many roundels in saltire argent, depicted upon a field argent'. Here, of course, were no colours or metals, but there were five small incised shields, each carrying the five *quinas* of Portugal, arranged in the form of a cross, with the lateral shields pointing into the centre, while surrounding the shield were ten castles and fleur-de-lis, the latter arranged in the form of a cross, while a royal cross surmounted all. King João II modified this coat of arms in 1485. On the shield he caused all the lateral castles to be made vertical, he removed the fleur-de-lis, and he reduced the castles on the surrounding ground to a number later fixed at seven. The coat of arms on the *padrão* erected at Cape Lobo was definitely of the old style, and thus was cut before May 1485.

This, however, would admit of the false date given by the sixteenth-century chroniclers, and the decisive evidence is to be found in the inscription itself, which ran:

ERA DA CREACÃ DO MŨDO DE SEIS MIL BJ^{c}LXXXJ ANOS DO NACIMENTO DE NOSO SENHOR JESHU DE MIL CCCCLXXXJJ ANOS O MUJ ALTO MUJ EICELẼTE PODEROSO PRINCIPE ELREY DÕ JOAM SEGUNDO DE PORTUGAL MÃDOU DESCO-BRIR ESTA TERRA E POER ESTES PADRÕES POR DIOGO CÃO ESCURDEIRO DE SUA CASA.

The translation would run as follows: 'In the year 6681 of the creation of the world, and 1482 of the birth of our Lord Jesus, the very high, very excellent and mighty prince King João II of Portugal ordered this land to be discovered and these *padrões* to be placed by Diogo Cão, squire of his house.'

The dating of the creation of the world follows the

chronology—generally accepted in the Middle Ages—of Bishop Eusebius of Caesarea (c. 260–341), who calculated that this event took place 5,200 years before the birth of Christ. The Bishop's years began, according to Byzantine practice, on the 1st September. The year 6681 accordingly corresponded to the period from the 1st September 1481 to the 31st August 1482, but the actual use of the date 1482 in the inscription further limits the period of Cão's departure to the first eight months of that year, for it seems clear that the inscription refers to the year in which he was commissioned and dispatched rather than to the years in which he erected the *padrão*.

It is likely that Cão's journey homeward was considerably quicker than his southward voyage, for both the current along the coast and the prevailing winds were in his favour. It is also likely that he sailed again to the Congo estuary to see whether his messengers had returned, and it may indeed have been on this occasion, rather than on his first visit there, that he took the four hostages. After leaving the river, he saved further time by sailing diagonally across the Bight of Biafra towards Mina, and there he discovered a picturesque, heavily-wooded, triple-peaked island of which the highest summit reached 1,500 feet—visible in clear weather for a good forty miles. It was New Year's Day, 1484, so he named the island Ano Bom; sixteenth-century cartographers were to honour him by calling it the Ilha de Diogo Cão, but later the name reverted to Annobon, as it appears on modern maps. After putting in at Mina for provisions and refreshment, and to learn the latest news of Portugal, Cão sailed out to sea for a good offing that would allow him to take advantage of the westward-flowing Guinea current. He probably steered west of the Cape Verde Islands and west of the Madeiras, and he reached

Portugal, to receive a hero's welcome, early in April 1484.

Certainly he was back by the 8th April, for on that day King João II signed a document in which he declared that Diogo Cão, *cavaleiro* of his household, had served him well in Guinea and other parts, and especially in the discovery of the new lands from which he had just returned. To reward him, and in anticipation of further services he was expected to render, the king granted Cão a pension of ten milreis a year to take effect from January 1484; the pension, which might pass to a son after his death, was to be paid by the treasurer of the Guinea trading house. On the 14th April João supplemented this grant by ennobling Cão and granting him a coat of arms, in consideration of the services rendered by his grandfather, Gonçalo Cão, and by Diogo himself, 'in the parts of Africa and of Guinea', in peace and in war, and especially for his services in Guinea where he had been sent on a voyage of exploration. The coat of arms consisted of a green field on which stood three rocks, each surmounted by a silver *padrão*; on each rose a blue cross, while the crest consisted of crossed *padrões*.

The report that Cão undoubtedly made to João has not survived, but it seems reasonable to assume that if he did not claim that he had rounded the continent, he at least assured the king that he had as good as done so. For on the 11th December following Cão's return, João's representative at the Holy See, Dr. Vasco Fernandez de Lucena, delivered a significant address to Pope Innocent VIII and his court. In the course of his oration, Lucena expressed the loyalty to the Papal See of 'the most serene and most illustrious prince, Dom João II, king of Portugal and Lord of Guinea, most holy son of Your Holiness'. He traced the history of Portugal and sang especially the praises of João II

who, he averred, had discovered more of the coastline of
Ethiopia in the four years, three months and thirteen days
he had been on the throne than his father had in forty-two
years. In the middle of the Ethiopias, the orator asserted,
João had ordered a castle to be constructed, at much labour
and great expense, of stone and lime, including stonework
transported from Portugal; it had bastions and moats, was
surrounded by a palisade and outer ditches, and lay close
to the gold mines. Thanks to this fortress a trade had been
established, so sacred, secure and considerable, that the
name of the Saviour, previously unknown there, was now
familiar to peoples who had originally been barbarous and
ferocious. Not only were Christians enriched by the great
abundance of gold and valuable commodities brought from
these parts, but the enemies of Christianity who inhabited
North Africa were now cut off from that lucrative trade.
Lucena then added—and this was a particularly significant
statement coming as it did so shortly after Cão's voyage—
that there was well-founded hope of exploring the Gulf of
Arabia, where there were Asian kingdoms and peoples,
known to Europeans through scanty and uncertain reports,
who scrupulously practised the Christian faith. If experienced
geographers could be believed, Lucena continued, Portuguese
navigators had approached to within a few days' voyage of
those parts. Already an immense stretch of the African
coast had been explored, and Portuguese seamen the previous
year had reached close to Promontorium Prassum where
the Gulf of Arabia began. They had explored the rivers,
beaches and harbours for a distance of more than forty-five
hundred thousand paces, all of which had been recorded
with the most exact observations of the seas, the lands and
the stars.

The only conclusion one can draw from such a statement

is that which Professor Damião Peres expressed in the small book on Cão which he published in Lisbon in 1957.

'For a man as experienced and cautious as João II to issue a statement in what was then the most important spiritual and political centre of Europe to the effect that Portuguese vessels had reached the waters of the Indian Ocean,' Professor Peres suggests, 'there must have been in his possession convincing evidence supplied by Diogo Cão and confirmed by the senior members of the expedition. Since we know that Ptolemy's Promontorium Prassum is in approximately the same latitude as Cape Santa Maria, and that a short distance beyond the latter, i.e. the farthest point reached by Cão on his first voyage, there opens out eastward a vast bay which is shown on Soligo's map [i.e. on the British Museum map entitled 'Ginea Portugalexe'], it is very probable that Diogo Cão and his men, misled by a stretch of coast they had not yet explored, became firmly convinced that they had reached the southern limit of the African continent, for the coast stretched out endlessly and was lost to sight in the East. And so convincingly must they have imparted this sensational news to the king that he accepted it as the truth, until Diogo Cão's second voyage came to shatter this attractive illusion.'

III

The Second Voyage of Diogo Cão

DIOGO CÃO set forth on his second voyage in 1485, probably at the end of the summer, and in command of two caravels. Our first-hand knowledge of this voyage is almost as scanty as that of its predecessor, for once again the royal instructions, and any log or journal that Cão may have kept, did not survive. We have to rely again on near-contemporary map-makers, on sixteenth-century chroniclers who are full in their references to some aspects of the voyage and tantalizingly silent on other important matters, and on the physical monuments which Cão left. These include not only two further *padrões*, but also a group of inscriptions cut on a cliffside at the falls of Yellala many miles up the Congo, which tell us the names of no less than eight of Cão's companions; three of them, Pero Escolar who piloted the *Berrio* in Vasco da Gama's expedition, Álvares who was master of da Gama's ship, the *São Gabriel*, and João de Santiago who sailed with Dias, were to play important parts in later voyages of discovery.

Despite the lack of direct evidence, one can safely assume that King João's instructions to his captain would have required Cão to take back the hostages seized on the first voyage, to recover the Portuguese messengers if they were still alive, to endeavour to establish communication with Prester John, and to complete the discovery of the sea route to India. On his way to the mouth of the Congo, Cão would certainly have called at the fortress of São Jorge de Mina, which had been completed since his first voyage and which was gathering not only many slaves for the Portuguese market but also such quantities of gold that the region around it would retain into the second half of the twentieth century the name of Gold Coast. The growing trade of Mina had led to more copious reports of the African hinterland, and as he paused there to renew his provisions and water, Cão would have heard the stories that were current there of a powerful king far in the interior, and these would have strengthened his hopes of establishing contact with Prester John or at least with one of his subject kings.

The hostages he carried back were, according to the chronicler Barros, men of good birth, a matter of importance in the Iberia of the day, where *fidalgos* enjoyed extraordinary privileges as compared with mere commoners; they had rapidly learnt the language and the customs of Portugal, and King João had ordered that they should be given presents to carry to the King of Congo, to whom they should also convey João's wish that the African monarch embrace Christianity.

When Cão reached the Congo and the local inhabitants saw that he had brought back their compatriots, and that these had been well treated, they gave him a cordial welcome. According to Barros, Cão sent one of the hostages to the King of Congo informing him of his arrival in the river, telling him that the caravels would continue their voyage southward along the coast, and asking that on his return the Portuguese messengers be waiting for him. On their safe delivery he promised to release the three Congolese hostages whom he had still not set free (a figure which suggests that there had been three Portuguese messengers). He added that on his return to the river he would seek conversations with the King. Apparently the King replied so promptly that the Portuguese messengers arrived in the charge of one of his captains even before Cão had departed southward; Cão immediately released the remaining hostages and entrusted the Congolese captain with rich presents for his king. Cão then departed on his exploration, and it was on his return voyage that he went inland to meet the King.

This is the account written by Barros in the 1530s, when men who remembered Cão's expedition would certainly be alive and when documents which have since vanished would still exist, and it is supported to some extent by the even earlier account of Rui de Pina, who was appointed royal chronicler-in-chief in 1497 and shortly afterwards began his *Croniqua del Rey Dom Joham II*, which was completed early in the sixteenth century, a mere twenty years or so after Cão had sailed though Rui de Pina made no reference to exploration south of the Congo. On these grounds the Barros account has been accepted by many scholars, but there are circumstances which have led others to regard it with doubt and to suggest that if Cão made a journey to the capital of the kingdom of Congo he made it before he proceeded southward. Their reasons are twofold. First, it is urged that King João must have been greatly excited to hear of the mighty river which Cão had discovered on his first voyage, and which might well be part of the inland waterway shown on Fra Mauro's map as leading to the lands of Prester John; it might even be possible to reach the Indian Ocean by way of the Congo and thus obviate a lengthy sailing around the extremity of the African continent, which Cão's first voyage had already shown to extend farther south than had been expected. Such considerations may well have led the King to instruct Cão to investigate these possibilities before proceeding southwards into unknown waters. An

even more potent reason for doubting the accounts of Rui de
Pina and Barros on this point is the evidence which suggests
that Cão may not even have been alive when the caravels
returned to the mouth of the Congo on their homeward
journey, and therefore could only have ascended the river
and left his name on a cliffside there on his southward voyage.

I shall leave the mystery of Cão's death to its proper place
in the narrative, but the very fact that there should be a
mystery of this kind makes it at least possible that, for
reasons it is now impossible to disentangle, the sixteenth-
century chroniclers presented an inaccurate ordering of the
events of Cão's second voyage, and with this possibility in
mind it seems appropriate to consider his journey up the
Congo as a self-contained episode before proceeding with
him on his coastal voyage to the south.

Whenever he set off, it would have been after midday,
when the sea-breeze begins to blow up the estuary of the
Congo. Leaving the cape that was crowned by the *padrão* of
his first voyage, he entered the river proper opposite
Bulambemba Point. The point and the sandy beach to the
north were white with surf, and behind the sand rose a line
of dark bush interspersed with palm trees. Beyond, up river,
the mangroves rose, oddly stilted, from their grotesque
adventitious roots. Only an occasional creek mouth broke
their dark green wall of foliage. The southern shore, three
miles away, presented a similar rampart of verdure, except
that in places leafy-topped white trunks towered high above
the mangroves. On this side too there were more openings
in the wall of vegetation. Occasionally a small clearing had
been made where ground rose above the ubiquitous mud, and
a hut, a dugout canoe or two, and a patch of yams or millet
revealed the presence of human life; behind the hut would
often rear the giant bole of a baobab tree. Behind the verges

of green, but nearer to the south than to the north, there were ranges of hills several hundred feet high.

The dry-season current of the Congo at this point runs at two or three knots, and whenever the sea-breeze dropped and they had to contend with both current and an outgoing tide, the caravels must have anchored; they would do this close in shore, since the depth of the Congo in midstream is still a hundred fathoms and more in its lower reaches, and the current carries floating islands dangerous to navigation, some of them supporting growing bushes and patches of papyrus reed.

Though the Portuguese after Cão traded on the river from the sixteenth century onwards, there was little travel upstream, and it was not until the nineteenth century that anything in the way of an adequate description of the river was written. In 1816 the British government sent Captain J. K. Tuckey to explore the Congo, and it is from the narratives of Tuckey and the other travellers who followed him after an interval of more than sixty years, such as the celebrated H. M. Stanley, and less well-known but vividly descriptive writers who arrived in the early 1880s, like the Rev. W. H. Bentley and H. H. Johnston, that we have to glean our impressions of the Congo as Cão and his companions must have seen it, for in those four centuries the river changed little. Only in the middle of the 1880s, almost exactly four centuries after Cão's journey up the river, did the impact of the west begin to affect the life of the river and to produce the conditions that inspired Joseph Conrad to write *Heart of Darkness*.

From Tuckey's account, the nearest in time to Cão's voyage, one gets a vivid impression of the sights and sounds that must have impinged upon the senses of the Portuguese mariners as they sailed in the evening up the wide lower reaches: the overhanging mangroves, the 'palm trees vibrating in the breeze', the 'immense flocks of parrots' that 'broke the silence of the woods with their chattering, towards sunset', and the low marshy islands, abounding in fishing eagles, terns and herons, off which it was customary to anchor at night.

Twenty miles up river from Bulambemba Point a barrier of islands appears to block the course of the river, but there are passes of varying depths along both the northern and southern banks. However, both the shapes of the islands and the depths of the channels between them change after every flood, and here Cão may well have hired the services of the local tribesmen who use the islands for the high-smelling occupation of drying shellfish.

Beyond these islands the tide becomes insignificant and the mangroves disappear. Palm trees become more numerous, and the forest presents an impenetrable front, thick with bamboo, rank with ferns and graced by brilliant orchids, while patches of reedy grass grow along the clay banks that line the main stream. The islands are no longer soft and marshy, but present solid banks of gravel and sand, covered with rank grass and weeds, often trampled flat by the hippopotamuses whose spoor mark the beaches. Eventually the forest thins out, and meadows of grass line the banks, their green broken by the flashing colour of clumps of hibiscus.

At the Fetish Rock (Pedra do Feitiço), which is a well-known mark for navigators on the river, the Congo narrows abruptly from twelve miles to a mile and a half wide where the Rock, a cliff-faced, isolated spur of granite a hundred feet high, projects into the stream from the southern shore and causes great eddies and whirlpools during the flood season. The Fetish Rock, to which the animist tribesmen attributed a special mana or sacredness, provides an excellent vantage point, and we can assume that Cão and his officers climbed it to survey the course of the river that stretched before them, running between two lines of hills, both of them almost bare of vegetation except for a few isolated baobab trees. On one of the hills to the north they would have noticed a strange and apparently natural structure which the local people called the *taddi engazzi*—the lightning stone; it consisted of a tall granite block, looking for all the world like a man-made tower, standing upon which rose another block, detached from the first but perfectly balanced.

Seven miles above the Fetish Rock, on a flat bench at the foot of the hills on the north side of the river, lies Boma, and immediately above it are the last islands of the Congo estuary, covered with dense bush and one of them rising to a height of 300 feet. Beyond the last island the river narrows to a single, impetuous channel, less than a mile wide. The banks are high and arid except where a patch of green indicates the entry of a tributary stream into the main river; above rise steep and treeless hills. The current runs swiftly, and where reefs and rocks project, there are risks at all seasons, though it is in times of high water, when many of the rocks are submerged, that travel here is particularly hazardous.

The perils of this deepening gorge, with its whirlpools and its rocks, with its swift current and uncertain breezes, made it a difficult place for caravels to manoeuvre, and it is fair to assume that Cão and his pilots, learning from the hostages and the local inhabitants that some leagues up river there were rapids which even a canoe could not ascend, decided to leave the caravels under guard at the village of Musuku, the beginning of an old trade route that ran south-eastwards to the *mbanza* of the King of Congo, and to continue their exploration up the river by small boat before making their way to the capital town. Doubtless Cão sent one of the hostages, with another Portuguese messenger, to inquire if his visit would be acceptable and to obtain a safe-conduct, and in the meantime proceeded by ship's boat or dugout canoe so that he could satisfy himself personally and report to King João that he had reached the limit of navigation and that there was indeed no easy waterway to the Arabian Sea.

Even if they hugged the bank as they followed the stream north-eastward, and thus avoided the worst of the currents, the boat-party would still have experienced increasing difficulty and danger, for whirlpools abounded, and at the end of the reach beyond Musuku they had to pass between two groups of dangerous rocks, one on each bank; the sound of the water breaking against the rocks on the south side could be heard for miles down river. At this point the valley turns south-east towards the village of Noqui, where the river again bends abruptly to the north and its valley becomes almost narrow enough to be called a canyon. Cão saw bare hills lining the eastern side, while on the west a wall of cliffs fell 800 feet sheer into the river—a spectacular sight, and for early travellers a gloomy one. The meanderings of the river continued with erratic abruptness, for after another two miles the valley swung sharply to the east, and a point on the inside of the curve constricted the stream to a width of less than half a mile, through which the water ran in high water as fast as eleven knots. Immediately opposite this constriction a bay had been gouged out of the rocky ramparts which has since become known as the Devil's Cauldron because of its furious eddies and violent whirlpools. It was no place that a caravel could have navigated, for steamers with a speed of ten knots have sometimes been unable to breast the current at this point, and it was a hazardous place even for a small boat; Captain Tuckey had to use a towing party on the bank wherever the lie of the land permitted and his craft were often whipped round and round in the whirlpools, which 'are formed in an instant, and subside as quickly'. When the Rev. Bentley travelled through in 1881, he described the loss of a canoe here in which six men had been drowned.

Like Tuckey, Cão seems to have negotiated the Devil's Cauldron successfully, and to have climbed the minor rapids above Matadi. But a mile and a half beyond Matadi lay the formidable barrier of the Lower Yellala rapids. These Tuckey found to consist of 'a ledge of rock stretching across the north shore about two-thirds the breadth of the river (which here does not exceed half a mile), the current breaking furiously on it, but leaving a smooth channel near the south shore, where the velocity of the current seems the only obstacle to the ascent of boats'. However, when Tuckey learnt that the major cataract at Yellala was 'a great perpendicular fall', and that the approach to it was far easier over land than by water, he decided to anchor his boats in a safe pool below the lower rapids and proceed by native paths. The same procedure was probably followed by Cão and his companions.

Tuckey felt that he had been misinformed by the Africans who had led him to expect something in the nature of a second Niagara. He found, as Stanley was to remark many years later, that the word 'falls' was rather a misnomer. 'It is', Stanley said, 'a series of vehement, rushing, tumultuous and vexed waters precipitated with remarkable force and energy, and seemingly eager to escape out of their constricted and deep mountain prison.' Tuckey saw the falls in the dry season and complained that, after all he had been told, it seemed like 'a comparative brook bubbling over its stony bed', but the Rev. Bentley, who saw the falls in the season of high water, was impressed by the way 'the river came down with a series of ten-foot leaps, plunging in wild waves at a high velocity, wave dashing upon wave, and throwing the spray far into the air. It is a struggle of water not to be surpassed on the face of the earth.' These observers were so taken up with the cascade itself that they did not pay much attention to its setting, but a more intimate view, which completes the picture of the spot as Cão must have seen it in 1485, was provided by another traveller of the 1880s, H. H. Johnston.

'The air in this gorge (from which the hills rise steeply to heights of fifteen hundred feet) is full of comminuted spray, maintaining a special vegetation. The rocks near the water's edge are covered with a long filamental waterweed of intense emerald-green which looks like tresses of long green hair. A plumbago creeper festoons the brows of the caverns which the water at some time or other has hollowed in the walls of stone . . . This creeper puts forth many tufts of bluish-white flowers. On the grey rocks large blue and red lizards chase flies that are basking in the sunlight, both lizards and flies being attracted by the native fishermen, who place wicker-work baskets and traps along the edges of the torrent to catch the fish that are swirled down the falls of Yellala.'

This was the spot to which Cão and some of his men penetrated in 1485, the limit of navigation on the Lower Congo, and an area which, though other Europeans may have visited it, none described until 1816. Here, on the rocks overlooking the swirling waters, Cão and his companions recorded the end of their exploration of the Congo and cut their names.

On a comparatively smooth-faced rock the explorers carved the royal arms of Portugal. Each escutcheon was

vertical, according to the new rules laid down by King
João II, so that the travellers must have left Portugal no
earlier than May 1485, and possibly later—a clear proof
that the inscription dates from the second and not the first of
Cão's voyages. To the right of the shield appears a large
cross, set on a conical base; the figure obviously represents a
padrão. Immediately to the right of the cross is an inscription
which runs

aq̃y chegaram os na
vios do escrecemdo
Rey dom joham ho se
g⁰ de portugall: d⁰ cãm:
p⁰ añes p⁰ da costa

which means: 'Here reached the vessels of the distinguished
King Dom João II of Portugal', and has the names of Diogo
Cão, Pero Añes and Pero da Costa added at the end.

To the right, on an adjacent face of rock, are the names of
Álvaro Pires and Pero Escolar (who was later to pilot the
Berrio in Vasco da Gama's expedition). Below the name of
Pires is the initial A with a stroke through one leg of the
letter. No one has explained this convincingly, though it had
been suggested that the crossing of the letter's leg was meant
to indicate a duplication of it—i.e. A.A., which might stand
for Afonso de Aveiro, but most scholars are justifiably
sceptical of this flight of imagination.

On a slightly lower face of the rock appear the names 'J⁰
de Samtyago D⁰ Pnro G⁰ Alvrz Antam'. Above the names of
Pinheiro and Álvares appears an inscription evidently cut at
a later time. In consists of a cross and the words 'da doesa g⁰
Alvz'. Used in such circumstances, a cross generally signifies
death, and the rest of the inscription means 'of illness,
Gonçalo Álvares'. Álvares was master of Vasco da Gama's

ship, the *São Gabriel*, from 1497 to 1499, so that he cannot have died on Cão's expedition; however, several letters of this inscription are more cursive than in the other names (notably the 'a' and the 'g') and the 'hand' is in a later style, so that the reference is evidently to a later expedition up the Congo on which Álvares met his death.

The chronicler Rui de Pina suggests and Barros insists that Cão went in person to visit the King of Congo, and it is likely that on his return from Yellala he disembarked at Musuku and followed the old trade route, which in fact was nothing more than a simple footpath, winding its way round boulders, termite mounds and trees, clambering up hillsides, plunging into valleys, seeking out fords to cross the intervening streams, and tenuously linking village and village. A later Portuguese official in 1881, when conditions had changed very little from those Cão endured, noted that it took thirty-five and three-quarter hours of actual travel to cover the ninety or a hundred miles from the Congo to São Salvador, by which name the King's city came to be known in the sixteenth century with the arrival of a Jesuit mission. (The town still stands, with the same name, in the northern part of Angola.) The journey could be covered in five days, but six or seven was more usual owing to the ardours of the mode of travel.

Cão's journey, with the armed men necessary to maintain his King's dignity and the native porters needed to carry provisions and gifts for the King and his courtiers, must thus have taken the greater part of a week each way. The day's march would start with the light of dawn, and on the first day the stony path switchbacked up and down over a succession of steep and barren hills. In places it crossed great slabs of smooth rock where the booted Europeans had difficulty maintaining their balance, and in the airless valleys the over-clothed Portuguese roasted in the heat reflected from the rocky hillsides. In the late morning the caravan would halt at some village, usually located on a smooth-topped hill close to a source of water, and there, in return for a present of cloth or beads or brass the headman would place a hut at the disposal of the strangers to rest during the heat of the afternoon.

By the second day the travellers passed into an area of lush forest inhabited by flocks of brilliant red birds with black necks, and on the third day they entered a fertile and populated region which was fed by many streams beside which grew trees with bright scarlet flowers. The narrow path made its way through grass that was often as high as fifteen or twenty feet, and the close walls of vegetation hindered the porters who carried their burdens in bales covered with palm-frond matting. In the early morning the plants were heavy with dew, and the travellers were quickly soaked to the skin, so that they envied the naked porters who were spared the discomfort of walking in wet clothes.

On the fourth or fifth day the travellers crossed the fourth of the steep ridges that lay between them and their destination, and descended into the valley of the Lunda, one of the tributaries of the Congo. Since Cão contrived to reach Yellala without mishap in the gorges of the Lower Congo, we can reasonably assume that he was not journeying in the season of the rains, when travel in the Lunda valley is extremely difficult because the rivers are swollen and floods spread over the low-lying ground which can be crossed only by rafts. In the season of low water the marshes could be crossed by causeways made of tree trunks laid in the water and covered with intertwined branches, and it is likely that Cão and his party crossed the Lunda River, which even in the dry season is a hundred feet wide, by one of the curious suspension bridges, constructed of twisted branches and hung from two anchoring trees, which were a feature of the region: he would probably have been delayed for a long palaver with the local chief or headman who demanded toll at such crossings. Down in the valley the nights were made almost unbearable by the falsetto whining of blood-hungry mosquitoes, whose silent sisters carried the malaria-causing parasites.

On the last day of the journey the path ascended a steep hillside where a precipice yawned on one side of the travellers; it crossed another wide valley, and then climbed to a ridge of high ground at the southern end of which lay the King's *mbanza*. This capital of the realm of Congo occupied a healthy site, well watered and admirably suited for agriculture, at an altitude of about 2,000 feet, between the Luebi and Coco Rivers, looking out over grassland, with the forest in the distance. It was a place that had long been inhabited and cultivated.

One can imagine Cão and the King meeting in the shade of one of those giant baobab or fig trees which were favoured sites for palavers, with the drums bellowing in the background and soft strains played on horns made out of whole tusks of ivory. Cão sings the praises of his royal master, boasts of his importance and tells of his noble intentions. The African King, in turn, informs his visitor of the greatness of the royal house of Congo, and tells of the half-legendary deeds of Ntinu Wene, the first sovereign, in the second half of the fourteenth century, who came to power in a chiefdom north of the Congo River, and expanded his dominions by conquest, absorption and migration, helped by his mastery of iron-making, which gave his people the best assagais for war and hoes for peace, and earned him the title of The Blacksmith King.

79

We can assume that on behalf of the Portuguese court Cão asked the friendship of this ruler whose authority was paramount over so vast an area (though it is likely that the King's authority no longer extended north of the Congo River). Cão must also have asked whether it was possible to navigate the Congo above the falls of Yellala so as to reach the eastern sea, and whether the King knew anything of a Christian potentate in the interior of the continent. In accordance with African traditions of hospitality, the King would undoubtedly have sought to please his guest by answering every question in the affirmative, but Cão probably received very little in the way of concrete information about the heart of Africa into which the Congo led, and he seems to have returned to his caravel convinced that the river provided no short cut to the lands of Prester John and to Asia beyond.

Whether or not Cão began his voyage southward from the Congo towards the extremity of Africa before or after his presumed journey to the court of the African king, it is likely that he coasted as quickly as winds and currents would allow to the seal-populated promontory where he had raised his last *padrão*. Beyond this monument, he skirted the great curve of the cliff-shored bay of Lucira Grande, and sailed on down a coast lined by red hillsides cut with valleys green with vegetation, until he was sailing by the arid land that lies around Moçâmedes in the south of Angola. One of the most surprising features of the early maps based on Cão's voyage is that none of them records the existence of Moçâmedes Bay, which Cão cannot have failed to observe, since it is eight miles across and bites a good five miles into the land. Moreover, there is a spectacular quality about its extreme desolation, for it is set in a northerly spur of the Namib Desert, and the only spot of greenery around the whole bay is where a stream-bed that occasionally carries water enters. Otherwise, there is no vegetation around Moçâmedes except for a few drought-resisting shrubs and the remarkable *Welwitschia mirabilis*, whose leaves may straggle ten feet across the ground. Behind the bay rise distant barren hills that gleam whitely in the afternoon sun.

It was ten leagues beyond this uninviting anchorage that Cão reached, in a setting of tall cliffs, with high hills rising in the hinterland, a promontory known as Cabo Negro which the *Africa Pilot* described as 'a remarkable headland, formed by a precipitous mass, upwards of 200 feet high, rising at the extremity of a low point, and resembling an island. It makes with a round, rugged, black face, whence the name . . .' It was an ideal setting for a monument that would visibly proclaim to all sailing along the coast that the King of Portugal had claimed it for his own, and Cão anchored in a bay to the north of the point, facing a beach that was overshadowed by a cliff whose upper strata projected over the shoreline. From this beach the limestone column was laboriously manhandled to the granite crest of Cabo Negro.

Only the weather molested this *padrão*; in 1892, when it was taken to the museum of the Sociedade de Geografia in Lisbon, its features were so worn that only indecipherable traces of an inscription could be seen on the shaft, which stood a shade over two metres high, and the royal coat of arms could barely be made out on the block that rose above it. However, it seems likely that, except for the change in the coat of arms which João II had ordered in 1485, and an altered date, the inscriptions on this column were identical with those on the almost perfectly preserved *padrão* which Cão had raised at Cabo do Lobo in 1483.

Not far south of Cabo Negro—or Monte Negro as it was

also named—Cão sailed into the natural harbour which today is known as Porto Alexandre. It is another of the rare spots on his voyage that are illuminated by a contemporary reference, for in his rutter compiled barely twenty years after Cão's voyage Pacheco Pereira included the following entry.

'Item. Eight leagues beyond Monte Negro lies a great bay which enters a league and a half into the land, and which is called the Angra das Aldeias (the Bay of Villages); and they gave it this name because when Diogo Cão discovered this coast by order of the king Dom João—may he rest with God —he found within this bay two large villages, and for this reason he gave it the said name. The negroes of this land are poor people who cannot maintain themselves or live except by fishing, of which there is much here; they are idolaters. In this land is no profit.' The bay of Porto Alexandre, where fishing by seine is still excellent, is the only break in the coastline large enough to correspond with Pacheco's Angra das Aldeias; it actually penetrates two and a half miles into the land, which appears to be less than the depth he gives (a marine league and a half would be four and a half miles), but his distances at this point are consistently exaggerated, for Porto Alexandre is in fact little more than three marine leagues south of Monte Negro.

Some writers have suggested that Porto Alexandre was also the Golfo do Salto (the Bay of the Assault) shown on early maps. The origin of the latter name is evident, for Barros mentions that during his voyage Cão made several sorties ashore for the purpose of kidnapping local inhabitants to be taken home to Portugal where they could be given Christian instruction and trained as interpreters, later being returned to their native lands. But it is quite clear from the Cantino map that the Golfo do Salto and the Golfo das

Aldeias (or Porto Alexandre) are two distinct features on the coast, the former lying farther to the south, at the entrance to the great Golfo das Areias (the Bay of Sands), which Pacheco Pereira calls the Manga das Areias (the Sleeve of Sands).

'Beyond the Angra das Aldeias', he says in his rutter, 'is found a bay which will be two leagues across at its mouth, which is called the Manga das Areias. It extends within the land five or six leagues, and at its mouth and from there within it has twelve or fourteen fathoms of depth. This land is desert and has no trees: it is all sand. Within this Manga is much fishing, and at certain times of the year there come here from the interior some negroes to fish, who make houses from the ribs of whales covered with seaweed and sand, and there they pass their unhappy life. This Manga das Areias . . . is situated 16½ degrees from the equinoctial line towards the antarctic pole.'

There can be no doubt at all of the identity of the Manga das Areias. At almost exactly the latitude given by Pereira—16° 31' to be exact—lies the tip of a long, low peninsula, on the east side of which lies the vast Baía dos Tigres—the Bay of Tigers or Leopards. This bay is nineteen miles long, with a breadth at the entrance of six miles; fifteen fathoms of depth can be found in its entrance, and nine miles in, the lead still shows ten fathoms. These measurements correspond remarkably closely to those given by Pacheco.

South of the Manga das Areias, nearing the southern confines of Angola, Cão sailed along a singularly featureless stretch of coastline, so devoid of landmarks that a single ten-foot rock receives attention in the pilot books. It was not merely a monotonous, but a hazardous coast, particularly for those who, like Cão, skirted it for the first time and without charts. The perils involved, even to mariners with modern ships and navigational equipment, are stated in almost minatory terms in the *Africa Pilot*, and merely to read of them in stark seamen's language suggests the risks which were involved in sailing two caravels along this coast.

'Heavy squalls and gales of wind are frequent, and often come on without warning, and with a cloudless sky. Sometimes sand is blown from the desert in large quantities, filling the air with minute particles, which are a long time subsiding; these conditions are accompanied by intense heat. The ordinary state of the atmosphere along this coast causes great refraction, and fogs are also frequent.' Even when there is no wind, there is usually a heavy swell. 'As the rollers frequently set in along this coast from the westward with great fury, and there is almost always a tremendously heavy swell thundering upon the shores, it is advisable to give the land a good berth, except in making the harbours.'

But this, with his explorer's mandate, Cão could not do. Yet at least, even though he was forced to sail fairly close in, he must have found that the great roar of the surf gave warning of the closeness of the shore. Most mornings he found himself facing a direct headwind, and doubtless stood out on a seaward tack, but in the afternoon the wind usually veers to the south-west, and with this change, on a landward tack, he would have been able to make southing. This stretch of coast the Portuguese pilots came to call the Mar Tenebroso (the dark and gloomy sea).

At one spot along it the early maps mark a Praia Verde— a green beach which Cão sighted and at which he perhaps landed. This can only be the mouth of the Cunene River, which now marks the frontier of Angola and South-West Africa. The river rises 746 miles away to the north-east, on the well-watered plateau near the town of Nova Lisboa in Angola, and flows southward before turning west and breaking through the arid mountains that parallel the Atlantic coast. When in 1824 Captain Chapman of the *Espiègle* visited the mouth of this river, the boat-party that ascended its course for a few miles was impressed by the height of the trees in the middle of this desert land and by the number of elephants and hippopotamuses they saw. Other travellers remarked that the beaches to the north of the river's mouth were strewn with trees, some of them still green, that had washed down in the rainy season; in the dry season, the river failed to reach the sea, but the islets at its mouth, still receiving fresh-water seepage, remained green and covered with vegetation throughout the year.

South of the Cunene, Cão sailed beside a desert coast, with dunes and sandhills rising behind the beaches, which were almost unbroken by headlands. Pacheco Pereira noted that this stretch of coast was very laborious to navigate, and that ships going to India in the early sixteenth century kept a good 250 miles out to sea. Indeed, for centuries after Cão first travelled there, the difficult wind patterns of the south Atlantic combined with the absence of material gain in this almost unpopulated land to keep ships away from South-West Africa. The Portuguese authorities ordered its exploration in 1520, but there is no evidence that this was done, and the first recorded survey took place in 1786 when Captain Thompson of the Royal Navy examined the coast to find whether it would be suitable for convict settlements, since the British colonies in North America were no longer available for that purpose. He reported the almost complete absence of fresh water, and his negative findings contributed to the establishment of Botany Bay as a penal colony, while South-West Africa was left in comparative isolation until the middle of the nineteenth century, when the exploitation of guano deposits, seal-skins and whale-oil caused ships to converge on what proved—until these resources were dissipated—to be a profitable coast. But for centuries after Cão first sighted it, his survey and the rutters based upon it remained the prime source of knowledge about this vast stretch of coastline.

The scattered names in Pacheco Pereira's rutter and on the early maps reflect the features of the coastline as Cão observed them sailing southward. There was another Cabo Negro; there was a region of dunes and shifting hills which the Cantino map appropriately called the Terra d'Areia, and southward of this Land of Sand a range of hills named the Serra de São Lazaro, which gives us one of the few points of chronological reference on this voyage; St. Lazaro's Day falls on the 17th December, and the year of observation was almost certainly 1485. 'All this coast is desert and without people', remarks Pacheco Pereira as he guides us southward in Cão's route, and the desolation impresses him so much that, coming to a tiny harbour where a few boats might shelter, he repeats it in almost the same words: 'and all this land is desert, for it is covered with sand.' Nothing has changed in nearly five centuries. Still, the *Africa Pilot* records: 'Flat rocky surf-beaten coast, with sandhills of moderate elevation extending as far as the eye can reach, continues mile after mile; varied occasionally by signs of vegetation in the form of the naras plant—a fruit-bearing creeper said to be a sign of the presence of fresh-water moisture.'

So featureless is the coast that even those places marked on the early maps are difficult to identify. It is impossible, for example, to pick out such spots as the Pŭta da Praia Ruiva (the Point of the Red Beach) or the Praia de Brançe, and even the little harbours to which Pacheco Pereira refers in his practical instructions for mariners are hard to identify. The Angra de Rui Pires, in which Pereira tells us that six or seven small vessels might anchor, may possibly be the mouth of the Hoanib River, while the even smaller Angra de Santo Amaro has been uncertainly identified as Ambrose Bay, which lies a little short of 21° south of the equator. The day of St. Amaro falls on the 19th January.

Pacheco Pereira goes on to tell us that twelve leagues south of Santo Amaro Bay lay the Angra das Areias (the Bay of the Sands), in latitute 22° 20' south, while ten leagues farther was the Cabo do Padrão, in latitude 22° 45' south. The land, he declares, is low and difficult to recognize, and it is safest to proceed by calculation of the latitude. This makes it somewhat ironical that his own latitudes for this stretch of coast are a degree out (perhaps owing to the error of his copyist), for the Cabo do Padrão, now known as Cape Cross, where Cão raised his last monument, is at 21° 47' south.

The *padrão* still stood on Cape Cross, in a good state of preservation, until on the 30th January 1893, after Bismarck had annexed South-West Africa, it was taken aboard the German cruiser *Falke* and transported to Kiel, where it was lodged in the Naval Academy. It was later removed to the museum of the Institut für Meereskunde in Berlin, which was later renamed the Institut für Physikalische Hydrographie. The museum building was destroyed by bombing on the 30th January 1944, and the restored *padrão* is now in the Museum für Deutsche Geschichte.

Pacheco Pereira describes the *padrão* as a pillar with three inscriptions, one in Latin, one in Arabic and one in Portuguese, all in the same tenor: that in the year so-and-so of the creation of the world, and in the year so-and-so of our Lord Jesus Christ, King Dom João II of Portugal had ordered that coast to be discovered by Diogo Cão, *cavaleiro* of his house and captain of his vessels. Pereira is approximately correct regarding the content of the inscription, but incorrect in his assertion that it is written in three languages. There are more or less identical inscriptions in Latin and Portuguese, but Arabic appears only in the dates given in Arabic numerals in the Latin inscription.

The form of the *padrão* is similar to that of the earlier ones, with a column and a superimposed block cut in one piece from the same slab of limestone and, above the block and fastened to it with molten lead, a limestone cross. The coat of arms of João II in the style he adopted in May 1485 appears on the front of the block. The inscriptions are cut on the reverse side of the block and round the column. They were transcribed and photographed by Professor Scheppig of Berlin on behalf of Luciano Cordeiro, the Secretary-General of the Geographical Society of Lisbon. The transcriptions ran as follows:

(A) mundi creatione fluxerunt anni 668? et (a) christi navitate 148? q(uum) (e)scelent(ssi)mus (s)erenissi(mus) que Rex d. Johannes secundus portugal(iae) per ia(co)bum canum ejus militem colu(m)nam hic situari jus(s)it.

and

Era da creação do mundo de bjm bj^c lxxxb de x$^{(to)}$ de llll^{c}lxxb o eycelent (e) esclarecido Rei dom J^o S^o de portugal mandou descobrir esta terra e poer este padram por d(^{o} c)ão cav^o de sua casa.

The Portuguese inscription ran:

In the year 6685 of the creation of the earth and 1485 after the birth of Christ the most excellent and most serene King Dom João II of Portugal ordered this land to be discovered and this *padrão* to be placed by Diogo Cão, gentleman of his house.

Scheppig was doubtful of his reading of the Arabic numerals in the Latin inscription; he wrote to Cordeiro that, in the fifteenth century, Arabic characters 'owing to their novel form, were still sources of frequent error and confusion'; it was difficult in particular, he remarked, to distinguish between a 4 and a 5. His preference was for 6684 and 1484. However, as Cordeiro and other scholars pointed out, these dates could not at first sight be reconciled with each other or with the Portuguese inscription, nor could they be reconciled with the style of the coat of arms. Certainly Cão was in Lisbon during the summer of 1484, while he disappears from history after 1485. Some early records asserted that the *padrão* on Cabo Negro was erected early in 1485. Cordeiro argued that the first date should be 6685; since the Eusebian year begins on the 1st September, this would have meant that Cão departed in the autumn of 1485, and not in 1484 as near-contemporary records suggest; and if he departed in 1484 it is impossible to explain why his *padrões* and his inscription on the rocks beside the Congo should have carried a coat of arms in a style introduced only in May 1485. Professor Damião Peres suggested a solution for the apparent conflict: he pointed out that the Latin *fluxerunt* referred to the year that had run its full course, while the Portuguese wording referred to the year in progress: both 6684 and 6685 were right; one date confirmed the other, and Cão left Portugal during the last four months of 1485. This was ingenious. But Professor Peres was inclined to accept the statement on the Behaim globe that the Monte Negro *padrão* was raised on the 18th January 1486. This would not have left sufficient time for the voyage to the Congo let alone any journey inland. And there would remain the problem of chronology arising from the names São Lazaro and Santo Amaro. It is safer simply to accept

Cordeiro's contention that Cão left after May 1485. If we accept the dedication to Santo Amaro to indicate the date of the discovery of the bay that was named after him, not far north of Cape Cross, then it seems likely that the *padrão* was raised in January 1486.

Though the general location of this last of Cão's monuments was known, its actual site was not re-established until my visit there in 1953, after I had worked on the problems relating to the exact places at which Dias turned back after rounding the Cape of Good Hope and where he erected his *padrões*. When they took down the *padrão* at Cape Cross the crew of the *Falke* raised a wooden cross on its site, and in 1895 the German authorities erected a replica, made of polished granite, with an added inscription and a large German eagle. However, doubt was later expressed as to whether this monument stood on the exact site of the original landmark, and in 1953 the Commission for the Preservation of Natural and Historical Monuments, Relics and Antiques of South-West Africa (which incorporated a representation of a *padrão* on its crest and letterhead) invited me to visit Cape Cross and inspect the site.

I consulted that indispensable handbook to coastal topography, the *Africa Pilot*, and found the following entry:

'Cape Cross is a point projecting about one mile into the sea, in the form of a truncated pyramid of moderate height, being the termination of, and connected by a low sandy plain to, the chain of red sandstone hills, which extend into the interior in an easterly direction, and form a good mark from seaward. The cape is low and of a red colour; it is difficult to distinguish, and from a distance appears like an island.'

Carrying in our minds this unspectacular description, my wife and I drove eighty miles northward from the coastal settlement of Swakopmund, passing many salt pans but little else on the way; indeed, there were places where the road itself was smoothly surfaced with salt. We eventually reached a sealing station two miles to the north of Cape Cross, and were soon made aware of our approach to the cape itself by the bellowing and barking of the sea-lions which crowded on the tip of the point so that it seemed to be convulsed with fur. On the landward side of this heaving mass jackals prowled in search of easy meals, while the white of the surf was speckled brown with diving and cavorting animals. South-east of the cape lay a salt pan which may once have been linked to the sea, and one could easily understand that off shore the cape might appear to be an island—and also why, on this featureless coast, Cão should have chosen it as the site for his farthest *padrão*.

The black granite replica, polished smooth by the sand-laden wind, stood boldly on the almost level expense of stone and sand. North-west of it a low mound was discernible, three metres in diameter, and rising a metre above the arid ground; the centre of the mound was ten metres from the replica.

This seemed a likely place to start my search with the assistance of men from the sealing station. First, I had the rocks that formed most of the mound removed. The majority of them could be rolled away by one man, but some needed two to lift them, and one, more than a yard across, demanded the combined efforts of three men and a crowbar. Now began the more delicate part of the search, as my wife and I systematically sieved the sand. On the surface, and for a few inches below, there were potsherds, fragments of ostrich shell, pieces of broken iron pots, and bones. There were no rocks in the centre of the mound, and here we sieved with particular care. Chips of pinkish crystalline limestone came to light which bore an unmistakable resemblance to the rock of which the Cão *padrões* had been composed and also to the two Dias landmarks which were known by 1953. Soon we exposed a socket which penetrated vertically into the mound. It narrowed to 30 centimetres at rock-bottom, and was 1·1 metres deep. In all, we recovered 103 limestone chips, and these had obviously been broken off the column as it was placed in the socket or as rocks were rolled against it to keep it upright. Some, perhaps, were also detached while it was being removed in 1893. These chips are now preserved in the museum at Windhoek, the capital of South-West Africa.

My visit to Cape Cross also led me to consider the mystery of Cão's death, which is linked with the identification of a certain Serra Parda (or dark range) that appears on the Martellus map already referred to and made in Florence in 1489. The Serra Parda is shown as lying to the south of Cape Cross, and is evidently one of the striking mountain peaks that rise behind this stretch of coastline. Clearly visible out at sea off Cape Cross itself is the massive Brandberg, which rises precipitously to an altitude of more than 8,500 feet; but the Brandberg lies to the north-east of Cape Cross; south of it, and to the south-east of Cape Cross the double peaks of the Spitskoppe are clearly visible from a ship sailing off shore. These lofty mountains rise up, a deep and conspicuous blue, in spectacular contrast with the yellow desert around them. They perfectly fit the description of a 'dark range'.

Off this stretch of the South-West African coast on the Martellus map there appears a highly interesting legend which runs:

'ad hunc usq. montem qui vocatur niger peruenit classis secũdi regis portugalie cui' classis pfectus erat diegus canus qui in memoriam rei erexit colũnam marmorea cum crucis in sign et ultra processit usq. ad Serram Pardam que distat ab mõte nigro mille miliaria et hic moritur.'

In his important study of the voyages of Cão and Dias which appeared in the *Geographical Journal* in 1900, E. G. Ravenstein translated the Martellus legend as follows:

'This mountain, called the Black Mountain [i.e. Monte Negro, in 15° 41' where Cão erected the first *padrão* of his second voyage] was reached by the fleet of [John] the second King of Portugal, which fleet was commanded by Diegus Canus, who, in memory of this fact, set up a marble column, with the emblem of the cross, and proceeded southwards as far as the Serra Parda, which is distant 1,000 miles from the Black mountain, and here he died.'

The cartographer was inaccurate in his distances (but so also, as we have seen, were the Portuguese transcribers of Pacheco Pereira). The actual distance between Cape Negro and Cape Cross, as Ravenstein calculated, is 435 nautical miles or 556 Italian miles. Nevertheless the distance on the Martellus map, if one measures it against the length of the Mediterranean shown there, does come to approximately 1,000 miles. A discrepancy in distance may well have been due to the haste and secrecy with which information was assembled to prepare a map in Italy by 1489, only three years after the voyage ended. But the statement of a fact like the death of Cão is much less likely to be inaccurate, since it is the kind of news that would have spread quickly among the navigators of Italy and other trading nations who were vitally interested in the Portuguese attempt to undermine the great Venetian trade with the East. The Martellus legend is strengthened by the fact that when Portuguese and Spanish representatives met at Badajoz in 1524 to establish where the line agreed under the Treaty of Tordesillas to divide Spanish and Portuguese rights on newly discovered lands would run on the opposite side of the globe, the Spaniards declared of Cão 'en otro viage desdel dicho Monte-Negro pasó á Sierra Parda, donde murió'; the Portuguese made no attempt to deny this assertion that Cão died at or near the Sierra or Serra Parda.

Last-ditch defenders of the theory that Cão actually returned to Portugal have brought forward arguments, based on dubious grammatical quibbles, that the inscription on the Martellus map means not that Cão died, but that the 'serra' died. Such arguments do not explain the difficult question of exactly how a mountain range can be thought to die, and the great majority of linguists agree that the inscription can mean only one thing; that Cão in fact died on his second voyage near the Serra Parda.

The only real difficulty about accepting this probability is that it runs contrary to the statement of the chronicler Barros that Cão visited the Congo on his return voyage. However, it seems likely that Barros may have been confusing two visits to the Congo, one by Cão and one by Dias. For they assert that the King of Congo sent back to Portugal with Cão a petty chief named Caçuto, who had been one of the hostages taken on Cão's first voyage, to act as his ambassador and to express his desire for priests to be sent to convert his people, for stonemasons and carpenters to build churches and houses, for herdsmen to domesticate livestock— and even for women to bake bread! His ambition was that his kingdom should resemble the Portugal which the hostages had described to him, and so with Caçuto he sent not only an entourage of headmen but also presents of ivory and palm cloth. But in fact, according to the chronicles, João II did not receive Caçuto until 1489, when he was baptized with much ceremony at Beja, returning to the Congo in December 1490. It is clear, then, that Caçuto could not have left the

Congo with Cão's returning expedition in 1486. Barros may be confusing Caçuto's visit to Portugal as an envoy in 1489, when he may well have been brought back by Dias, with his first visit in 1484 when he was taken there as a hostage by Cão. Certainly Cão cannot have taken him the second time, and this leaves us free to assume that Cão's journey up the Congo was made on his southward voyage, that he did indeed die some time early in 1486 as he was beginning his exploration south of the *padrão* at Cape Cross, and that on his death his companions decided to turn homeward. It is significant that at this point Cão disappears entirely from history; it seems inconceivable—had he returned to Portugal—that no reference should survive, in chronicle or document or local tradition.

Yet there is no certainty in the matter, although, for a brief while on my visit to the site of the *padrão* at Cape Cross, I imagined it might be established. After we had finished our excavation there, an employee of the sealing station told me that some two hundred yards to the west of the German replica I would find the graves of some Portuguese sailors who long ago had landed there from a ship, which had been forced to put out to sea by bad weather and to abandon the men to their fates. There was no indication who the men were or how they had died or who had buried them, and even as the story was told me I was puzzled as to how the tradition might have been transmitted from a distant past in a region now devoid of indigenous inhabitants. However, I had no intention of leaving any possible clue to Cão's fate uninvestigated, and I excavated one of the mounds; it consisted of nothing but sand and rocks. At this point I realized that an old resident of the sealing station seemed to be gaining a great deal of amusement from my labours. When I questioned him, he told me that he himself had helped to construct the mounds almost forty years before; they were the remains of defences which he and other Germans had built in 1914 against the possibility of a British landing in the shallow bay to the north of Cape Cross on which the sealing station was situated. He pointed out the remains of a light railway which had been built to remove guano and later to establish and supply the military post. At this point one of the labourers at the sealing station, an Ambo tribesman, volunteered the information that he knew the site of two real Portuguese graves. I went to the spot he indicated. The mound I decided to excavate was a satisfactory six feet in length and five across; it rose a foot above the ground. I removed a layer of stones and rocks from the top, and a thickness of sand, and then my spade uncovered what was obviously brown hair. I looked down with considerable excitement at what might be the remains of the great Diogo Cão—for in that dry sand a substance like hair might be preserved for centuries. My excitement waned as each spadeful disclosed more hair, and then large and obviously unhuman bones. It was, I recognized, the grave, not of a man, but of a sea-lion which for some ritual purpose had been buried by a tribe unknown. I departed, having failed to solve the enigma of the fate of Diogo Cão.

IV

The Outward Voyage of Bartolomeu Dias

WHEN the survivors of Cão's expedition returned to Portugal and made their reports to King João II, he was bitterly disappointed that none of the principal objectives of the voyage had been achieved: the supposed channel through Africa to the Arabian Sea had not been found, no contact had been made with Prester John or any of his subject kings, and still the southern extremity of Africa had not been rounded. Nevertheless, the King persisted in his intent, and ordered that immediate preparations should be made for the exploration along the African coast to be continued.

To command the expedition he chose Bartolomeu Dias, granting him an annuity of six milreis 'for services to come'. Very little is known of the early life of Bartolomeu Dias. He was, at the time of his appointment, a gentleman at the King's court, but as he had more than one namesake among the pilots and captains who were active at the same time, it is often difficult to establish when a contemporary reference to a Bartolomeu Dias is actually a reference to the explorer. He may have been the man exempted in 1478 from dues on ivory imported to Portugal from Guinea; he may have commanded a ship in the flotilla which Azambuja took with him in 1481 when he founded the fortress at Mina. Certainly he must have had a past of distinguished and resourceful service to be given an appointment so vital to the achievement of Portuguese commercial, territorial and missionary ambitions.

The squadron which Dias commanded consisted of three ships. Two of them were caravels of about 100 tons. The third vessel, intended as a storeship, was somewhat larger; she was probably a *caravela redonda*, rigged with a square mainsail. Each vessel would certainly have been provided with copies of the latest charts, embodying the discoveries of Cão's two voyages, and with astrolabes, quadrants and declination tables to enable the pilots to calculate latitude by observing the height of the sun and of prominent stars. Revolutionary developments in astronomical navigation were at this time being pioneered by the mathematicians employed by the Portuguese court.

As pilot in his flagship (whose name has not survived), Dias took with him Pero de Alenquer, who appears to have distinguished himself already as a navigator, for in 1483 King João gave him special permission to wear garments of silk, normally forbidden to men of his rank by the strict Portuguese sumptuary laws, and to wear a seaman's whistle suspended from his neck by a gold chain. The second caravel, the *São Pantaleão*, was commanded by João Infante, and her pilot was Álvaro Martins. The storeship, whose name is also unknown, was under the command of Diogo Dias, a brother of Bartolomeu; her pilot, João de Santiago, had accompanied Diogo Cão and ascended the Congo with him. As well as their crews, the ships carried six Africans who had been taken to Portugal—some of them by Cão—from the shores of Guinea and Angola. They were to be landed at various spots on the coast, with samples of gold, silver and spices and orders to inquire where such products were to be found in those areas; they were also to sing the praises of the King of Portugal, and to explain to local chiefs and kings that he

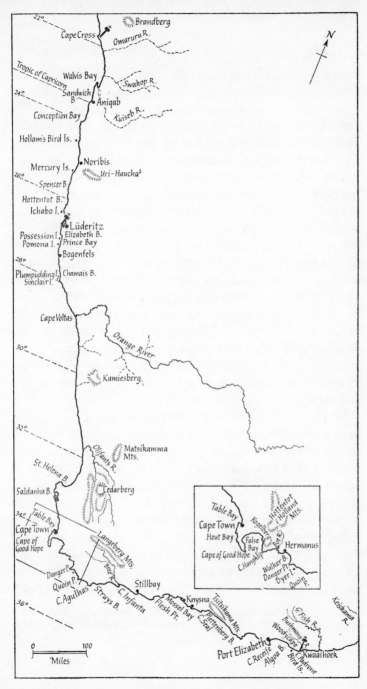

3. South Africa coastline, Cape Cross to the Keiskama River

wished to establish relations with Prester John, the Christian King of Abyssinia, and to discover the way to India. Some of these Africans were women, for the Portuguese court trusted that the local inhabitants where they were landed would treat them with chivalry; one can only hope that there was no rude disillusionment.

The royal instructions which were issued to Dias have vanished and so have all the actual records of his voyage, like those of Cão's. Again, we have to rely mainly on contemporary and near-contemporary maps and chronicles. Even the sites of two out of the three *padrões* which Dias erected were lost when I began my own researches in 1935, and that of the third was not clearly established, so that where Dias turned back on his journey home and the exact extent of his exploration were still a matter of conjecture. In the following chapter I shall tell the story of the discoveries by which I solved some of these problems; in the present chapter I shall tell the story of Dias and his outward journey as it could then be reconstructed from the literary and cartographical evidence.

Dias sailed from the Tagus in August 1487. It is true that Barros, and António Galvão who wrote in 1563 and probably accepted the statements of the earlier chronicler, both declared that Dias weighed anchor in August 1486, while Barros added that Dias returned in December 1487 after a voyage of sixteen months and seventeen days. However, this is one point on which contemporary evidence is fairly strong, and all of it tends to disprove the dates given by Barros in 1539. Towards the end of the nineteenth century attention was drawn to certain marginal notes written by hand in two books once owned by Christopher Columbus.*

* 'Nota quod hoc anno de .88. in mense decembri apulit in vlixiponam bartholomeus didacus capitaneus trium carauelarum quem

One of these notes stated that Dias reported to his king in 1488; another stated that it was in December 1488 that Dias returned to the Tagus. These dates are borne out by the evidence of Pacheco Pereira, who deserves special attention because he wrote from direct experience; Dias rescued him on his return voyage, and Pereira must have had very vivid recollections of his own ordeal when he wrote the *Esmeraldo de Situ Orbis*, in which he records that Dias raised his farthest cross in 1488 and in the same year discovered and named the Cape of Good Hope. Finally, at the meeting of maritime experts from Spain and Portugal which took place at Badajoz in 1524, and to which we have already referred in connection with the death of Cão, 1488 was mentioned—without disagreement—as the year when Dias made his discoveries.

On his way southward Dias would have called at São Jorge de Mina on the Gold Coast to replenish provisions and to allow his men to refresh themselves before voyaging into unknown waters. Beyond the Congo, as the chroniclers say, he 'counted the *padrões*', and in a suitable bay somewhere in South-West Africa he transferred provisions and other

---

miserat Serenissimus rex portugallie in guinea ad tentandum terram & renunciauit ipso senerissimo rex prout nauigauerit ultra yan nauigatum leuche .600. videlicet .450. ad austrum et .250. ad aquilonem vsque vno promontorivm per ipsum nominatum cabo de boa esperança quem in agesinba estimamus quique in eo loco inuenit se distare per astrolabium vltra linea equinociali gradus .45. quem vltimum locum distat abvlixbona leuche .3100. quem viagium pictauit & scripsit de leucha in leucha in vna carta nauigacionis vt occuli visui ostenderet ipso serenissimo regi in quibus omnibus interfuit.' (In *Imago Mundi*, by Pedro de Ailly, facsimile in *Racolta Colombiana*, part I, vol. III, pl. LXX, transcribed by A. Fontoura da Costa, *Ás portas da Índia em 1484*, p. 52.) A translation appears below, p. 175. The second note (in 'Historia rerum ubique gestarum de Pio II', facsimile in *Racolta Colombiana*, part I, vol. III, pl. XL, also transcribed by Fontoura da Costa, p. 52) ran 'Serenissimo Regi Portugallie renunciatum fuit ab vno suo capitaneo anno de .88. quem miserat ad tentandum terram in guinea quod nauigauit vltra equinocialem gradus .45..'

supplies from his storeship and left it at anchor with a care-taker crew of nine men while the two caravels sailed on towards the extremity of Africa.

It was once assumed that Dias left the storeship at the bay he named after St. Christopher but which now bears the name of the Bremen merchant F. A. E. Lüderitz who played so great a part in the German annexation of South-West Africa. However, as the Portuguese scholar Viriato Campos pointed out as recently as 1966, there are good chronological and other reasons for rejecting this assumption. Dias—as we shall see—named his first newly discovered land, not far south of Cape Cross, on the 4th December 1487. He raised his third *padrão* at Lüderitz on the 25th July 1488, less than eight months later. But according to Barros, Dias was away from the storeship for nine months, which means that he must have continued northward from Lüderitz into a region already discovered by Cão before he rejoined it. This, Campos suggests, would represent a logical course of action, for it would obviously be wise for Dias to leave the ship in a harbour already recorded by Cão, since there was no guarantee that he himself would discover another sheltered anchorage.

Campos therefore suggests that the storeship waited in either the Angra das Aldeias (Porto Alexandre) or the Manga das Areias (the Baía dos Tigres), both on the coast of present-day Angola. At Porto Alexandre there is good fishing and water can be found at the south end of the bay by digging a few feet into the sand. But the Baía dos Tigres, apart from lying farther south and therefore being nearer to the objective of the voyage, is also better watered, while an American captain named Morrell who went there in 1829 described it as one of the best places in the world for netting fish; the region was certainly capable of supporting life, for Morrell found a village ten miles from the coast in a valley where the springs never dried up even in the most severe of droughts. Viriato Campos appears to favour the latter site because Pacheco Pereira, as we have seen, tells how the people from the interior—presumably from Morrell's village—came to the bay at certain seasons to fish, and this, Campos argues, implies that at some time the Portuguese were in the bay long enough to observe native habits over an extended period. This he regards as an indication that the storeship anchored here. However, it must be borne in mind that Barros, inaccurate in some other matters, may not be correct in his figure of nine months, and that the Portuguese might easily have learnt of fishing trips made by tribesmen from the interior from the natives of this region whom Cão took captive. In other words, the question of which harbour Dias used to shelter his storeship is still undecided, though the Manga das Areias (the Baía dos Tigres) is doubtless the most likely candidate.

Beyond Cape Cross and the Serra Parda the two caravels made a close coasting and on the 4th December Dias bestowed on the land he was passing the name of Santa Barbara; three days later, on the 7th December, he named a point after St. Agatha. Again, on this almost featureless coast, it is difficult to identify the names that appeared on late fifteenth-century maps as a result of Dias's observations. The Praia das Verdes (Beach of Verdure) may well be the shallow bay at the mouth of the Swakop River which later travellers described as being green with reeds, but the Praia das Aves (Beach of Birds) could refer to almost any beach in South-West Africa, where the sands are so often white with gulls and the shallows black with cormorants. But an element of certainty appears when we reach the Golfo da Conceicão, named on the 8th December, which cannot be other than modern Walvis Bay, protected by its five-mile-long peninsula.

Dias would undoubtedly have anchored in this excellent harbour, sheltered from the wind and the rolling Atlantic waves. 'There is a broad sandy beach round the bay, and sand hills heaped up in various forms inland, and the general look of things here is very wild and Arabian-like,' said James Alexander who visited Walvis Bay in 1837 and saw a scene completely unchanged since Dias first discovered it. 'The quantities of sea fowl we saw on the shores of the bay, winging their way, and screaming over its green waters, were immense,' Alexander continued; 'pelicans with snow-white plumage, and a slight blush of red on the wings, appeared in vast flocks; flamingoes with outstretched necks and drooping bills, stalked along the beach, and allowed us to approach them; wild geese in long strings flew overhead . . . and sand-larks . . . hurried along the wet sand before us.' Like Alexander 300 years afterwards, Dias and his men may have seen here the furtive Bushmen, short and sparse of form, tawny-coloured, the men armed with bows and poisoned arrows. Or, like Morrell, they may have encountered the Hottentots who lived in villages near to Walvis Bay, and whose way of life did not change significantly until the late nineteenth century. Their wealth consisted of cattle and sheep, and they lived in conical structures of poles almost like wigwams, and covered with bullocks' hides, but their sustenance came mainly from the sea; with their sixteen-foot lances they could spear seven- or ten-pound fishes at a distance of thirty yards and arrows shot from their longbows could drop a gull on the wing at a distance of fifty yards. They had a technique of drying and preserving seabirds so that their flesh lost all taste of fish and could be kept for a whole year. Dias may well have traded in barter for such dried birds to supplement the rations of his crews.

Travelling ever southward, Dias named on the 21st September the Gulf of St. Thomas, which is probably present-day Spencer Bay in Namaqualand, flanked by a prominent cliff to the north and to the south by a headland which rises to a height of more than 600 feet and which is the most remarkable landmark on this desolate stretch of coast. The Bay of Santa Vitoria, as Dias named it, is probably Hottentot Bay, dominated by another 600-foot cliff, and an unnamed island that appears on Cantino's map is undoubtedly Ichabo, not far to the north of Lüderitz. Between Ichabo and Lüderitz the coast presents a forbidding appearance: rocks and reefs extend far out to sea, while the rollers often break as far off shore as the ten- or twelve-fathom line. These rocks and reefs are represented on the Cantino map, which then marks a vast bay, studded with islands, the Golfo de São Cristovão. There can be no doubt that this is what Pacheco Pereira described as 'the beautiful Angra das Voltas (Bay of the Tacks) which has a large mouth facing the north-west; and this . . . Angra das Voltas enters within the land a good league and a half, where a hundred vessels can anchor in ten or twelve fathoms, secure in all weathers. This bay is a league or more across; and it has within it some rocky islets, and there is much fishing here. This bay was discovered by Bartolomeu Dias . . . It is situated in latitude 29° 20′ south. This land is bare and without any trees at all.'

As so often happened, either Pacheco Pereira's latitudes on this stretch of coast are sadly out or his copyist erred. There is only one bay to which this description can apply, and this is the bay considerably to the north of 29° 20′ to which the ridiculously inappropriate name of Angra Pequena (Little Bay) was applied in the early nineteenth century and which was later named after the German merchant Lüderitz.

The bay was named the Angra das Voltas, according to Barros, because of the number of tacks that were necessary to enter it; Dias stayed for five days because of the weather which would not permit him to continue on his voyage. It is likely that a fresh southerly wind was blowing, and that tacking into the bay was indeed laborious; once within its shelter he would have waited for a change in the weather before proceeding. Barros adds that the first of the negresses brought from Portugal was put ashore at the Angra das Voltas, and the museum in Lüderitz contains the skeletons of three negresses, excavated locally, which are alleged to be the remains of the unfortunate women landed by Dias. But the claim is without proof and improbable; in any case, the number of skeletons is excessive. As we have seen, it used to be generally assumed that it was here that Dias left his storeship, but if this had been the case it is surprising that Barros did not record it specifically and, as we have seen, there is now good reason to assume that the storeship lay in a more northerly anchorage.

When the wind changed and he could leave the Angra das Voltas, Dias sailed southward through a sea studded with rocks (one of which was pierced by a remarkable natural archway a hundred feet high) and with many islands and islets, all of them white with the guano of innumerable seabirds. It was the end of the nesting season, and Dias and his men doubtless feasted on eggs and birds alike. There followed a particularly inhospitable stretch of coast, flanked by barren and forbidding sand dunes which rose to a height of 500 or 600 feet, and then, on the 26th December, they sailed into the Golfo de Santo Estevão, which was probably Elizabeth Bay.

On the last day of 1487 Dias sailed beside the featureless coast north of the Orange River, which he named the Terra de São Silvestre, but he apparently passed without noticing it, the mouth of the Orange River itself, which now marks the boundary between South-West Africa and the Cape province of South Africa. Either the summer rains in the far interior had not yet brought down the floods that at certain seasons discolour the sea many miles off shore, or the surf breaking on the shoals that extend six miles out to sea (named Bramidos or The Roarings in early maps) caused the caravels to give this part of the coast a wide offing.

Southward the coast was still rocky, though here and there would be a beach backed by sandhills on which the vegetation became increasingly more abundant. Spectacular mountains caught the eyes of the voyagers, like the lofty Kamiesberg, 5,500 feet high, which lies forty miles inland but is clearly visible from off shore and which is probably the peak that Dias named the Lombada da Pena. The first of two rivers which are marked on the early maps as Rio do Infante was named here; it is probably Olifants river, and was doubtless examined by João Infante, the captain of the *São Pantaleão*. On the Feast of Epiphany, the 6th January, Dias named the Serra dos Reis—the Range of the Kings, and this can probably be identified with the very prominent Matsikamma mountains in 31° 40′ south; these mountains, which form the northern extension of the Cedarberg, have flat tops flanked by precipitous walls of rock and present to the north-west, from which side Dias would have seen them, particularly steep and striking red cliffs.

Beyond the Serra dos Reis, Barros tells us, the caravels lost sight of land owing to a storm that lasted for thirteen days and drove them with their sails at half-mast through cold and dangerous seas. However, as E. G. Ravenstein has pointed out, northerly gales are extremely rare in these waters in January, which is the middle of the southern summer, and squalls from the north-north-east and north-north-west, which do sometimes blow at this season, are always of short duration. Admiral Gago Coutinho, the Portuguese maritime authority, suggests that it is more likely that Dias tired of beating against the prevailing southerly winds and deliberately stood out on a tack to sea. After some days, during which they may indeed have reached the roaring forties and entered seas that were really cold and dangerous, the explorers steered east, and found no land. Dias then ordered the course to be set to the north, and very soon his mariners joyfully hailed the land.

It was the mouth of a river along whose banks the cattle were grazing, tended by so many herdsmen that Dias called it the Rio dos Vaqueiros; today it is called the Gouritz River, but the point to the east of it still bears the name Cape Vacca. Because of the heavy surf it was impossible to get a boat ashore, so the caravels continued along the coast. To the joy of all, it ran almost due eastward; it appeared to Dias and his men—and indeed correctly—that at long last the continent of Africa had been successfully rounded.

By now it was already February, and as the caravels sailed past a line of cliffs which culminated in a rocky bluff pierced by a great cave, Dias named it after São Bras, whose festival falls on the third day of that month; the name was later anglicized to St. Blaize. The cape provided shelter on the western side to a broad expanse of water, which Dias also named after São Bras, but which the Dutch were later to call Mossel Bay.

For several years the Angra de São Bras became a regular calling place for Portuguese ships bound for the Indies, and Pacheco Pereira devotes considerable space in his rutter to a vivid description of the spot—written only seventeen years afterwards—as Dias and his men must first have seen it, populous with sea-lions and seabirds.

'Within this bay is an islet close to the land on which are many very large seals which have shoulders and necks and manes like lions. Also on this islet are many seabirds, larger than ducks, covered with feathers, but without any plumes in the wing, so they cannot fly, and those who hear the voice of these birds think that it is an ass braying [it is known today as the jackass penguin]. This bay is sheltered from all winds except from the east-north-east to the south-west which blow across the bay and raise a great sea when they blow with force. On the west side of this bay is a point of land with some rocks which resemble islets when you come in from the sea, and one of these rocks looks like a small turretted castle. This is the first thing you see when you reach the bay. And this point is slightly more than a cross-bow shot in length. And from the said point there projects into the sea a reef of rocks on which the sea when rough breaks for a distance of a quarter of a league; it almost closes the mouth of the bay. And above this point of low land a range of hills comes down to the edge of the sea.'

Pacheco Pereira goes on to tell of the little river that flows into the bay, and to remark, with a touch of nostalgia, that beside it 'grow many reeds, rushes, mint, wild olive trees and other plants and trees like those of Portugal'. Apart from the fact that the river meant fresh water and its trees meant firewood, one can imagine the pleasure that Dias and his men must have gained, after the pestilential coasts of Guinea and the desert shores of south-western Africa, to find themselves once again in a temperate climate and a green landscape. Pereira recommended an anchorage a little over a quarter of a league from the shore, in four and a half fathoms of water (in what today is known as Munro Bay) and there Dias actually anchored. He immediately sent his men ashore to seek fresh water and to establish contact with the local inhabitants who, he was delighted to observe, possessed herds of both cattle and sheep.

By the time Pacheco Pereira wrote, the local Hottentots (for the Bantu-speaking tribes had not moved as far west as this in the southern extremity of Africa) had become accustomed to the visits of Portuguese ships, and traded their cattle, sheep and goats for such goods as brass basins, bells and red cloth; they had also won a reputation for untrustworthiness, and Pereira warns that 'whoever goes to this place must beware of the negroes of this land because they are very bad people, and several times they have tried to kill the crews of ships which go there, and he who goes ashore should always be on his guard.'

The fatal chain of distrust that led to this situation may have its beginning in that very first encounter between Europeans and Hottentots when Dias landed at Mossel Bay. The Africans were astonished at the Portuguese ships and at the extraordinary garb of the white men; Dias and his men in turn looked with interest on the Hottentots, whom Álvaro Velho, a member of Vasco da Gama's expedition which reached the bay only nine years later, described as being of a chestnut colour, comparatively small in stature, with fuzzy hair, dressed in skins and wearing bracelets of elephant hair and ivory. Velho remarks that they carried assagais of wild-olive wood hardened in the fire and bows and arrows, and their cattle were magnificent wide-horned and humped beasts as large and succulent as any animal that could be seen in Portugal. In Vasco da Gama's presence four or five of them pulled out reed flutes 'and some played high and some played low, harmonizing together very well for negroes in whom music is not to be expected; and they danced like negroes.' But the dancing and the music ended and misunderstanding followed; the Hottentot warriors seemed to be threatening da Gama's men, and he fired a couple of small guns at them and put them to flight.

A similar and more tragic incident abruptly ended the visit of Dias to Mossel Bay. At first, after the initial astonishment, the Hottentots crowded round to receive the trinkets which the Portuguese offered them. Oxen and sheep were bought by barter so that the Portuguese enjoyed their first fresh meat for many weeks. Then they started filling their water casks at the mouth of the little river that flowed into the bay. Suddenly, for some reason which the Portuguese could not understand, the Hottentots began to throw stones from the low hill that overlooked the watering place, and Dias, in his annoyance, snatched up a cross-bow and shot one of them dead. Then he and his men appear to have withdrawn immediately to their ships and continued their voyage.

The caravels sailed eastward along a coast fringed with sandy hillocks; rocky shores appeared, alternating with sandy beaches, while in the interior a lofty mountain range rose into view; it reminded some of the mariners of the highest range in Portugal, and so they christened it the Serra da Estrela. Off one headland—possibly the rocky Gericke Point—the seamen caught many fish and so gave it the name of Pescaria. The look-outs in the crow's nests sighted inland lakes, and the caravels sailed past red cliffs and bush-covered bluffs and grass-green headlands, and then sighted a remarkable cape that looked like an island fringed by overhanging cliffs; called Cape Talhado by its discoverer, it has become the Cape Seal of today, aptly named, since the bay beyond—which Dias named the Baía das Alagoas and which is now Plettenberg Bay—was alive with marine mammals and seabirds.

From this point the coast began to trend south of east, and this must have dampened the spirits of the explorers, bringing doubts into their minds as to whether they had indeed rounded the point of Africa. Otherwise, it was an excitingly spectacular stretch of coast, much of it lined with cliffs between 300 and 600 feet high and broken by forest-filled gorges leading inland towards the massive Tsitsikama mountains which reared in the distance. To the east these mountains dwindled in height until they ended in a low point which was later named after St. Francis, but which Dias called the Ponta das Quiemadas because of the grass fires which were sweeping along it towards the mountains. The sandy bay beyond was lined by pastures filled with herds and herdsmen, and hence the early voyagers called it the Golfo dos Pastores. The rocky coast that followed this bay culminated in the Cabo da Roca, the Cape of the Rock, which later acquired from the shoals that fringe it the name of Cape Recife—the Cape of the Reef.

Around this cape lay a broad bay which Dias called the Bay of the Rock; later it took the name of Baía da Lagoa from the lagoons at the mouth of the Swartkops River, and this in turn was corrupted to Algoa Bay. It was here that Port Elizabeth would be established by English settlers coming to Cape Colony in 1820. The caravels anchored in the bight of the bay, in the lee of the largest of three rocky islets. It was about half a mile each way, and 200 feet high; the lower slopes were brown with sea-lions and the summit white with birds. Led by Dias, a party of Portuguese landed, and toiled up the sides of the islet, pushing aside the animals which made more noise than the crowd at a bullfight, and dragging a wooden cross which they erected on its

v The inscription at the Yellala Falls, at the head of the estuary of the Congo, recording the visit by Diogo Cão

VI The stone cross raised by
Diogo Cão at Cape Cross
in South-West Africa

VII The Dias pillar from Kwaaihoek,
as reconstructed

crest. In the shadow of the cross they celebrated mass, and named the islet ilhéu da Cruz.

From this point the coast now appeared to be running consistently eastward again, and at this point, according to Barros, 'as all the people were very weary and frightened from the great seas they had passed through, all with one voice began to complain and to demand that they should go no farther; they said that as the provisions were almost exhausted they should turn and search for the storeship which they had left behind and which was already so distant that when they reached her they would all be dead from hunger. How then could they sail any farther?'

Dias called a meeting on shore that was attended by the captains, pilots and masters and by the leading seamen. He made each man swear an oath to give the best and most honest council of which he was capable. Everyone agreed that they should turn back, and a document was drawn up in which this opinion was expressed, and which each proceeded to sign. But Dias, desiring to continue the exploration, finally persuaded them to continue for another two or three days along the coast. He promised that at the end of this time, if they found nothing that might compel them to continue, he would comply with their advice and turn for home.

The caravels raised their anchors and sailed round Algoa Bay, past a long, sandy beach backed with sand dunes and hills covered with dense bush. At the eastern end of the bay, twenty-six miles east of the ilhéu da Cruz, stood a rocky headland faced with sandstone cliffs, and four or five miles south of this cape the heavy surf betrayed the presence of a group of rocks and islets which from their lowness and flatness Dias named the ilhas Chãos; today they are known as the Bird Islands.

At the end of the stipulated term of days, the caravels reached a river where, according to Pacheco Pereira, João Infante was the first person to leap ashore, and so this river, like an earlier one, came to bear his name. Doubtless the rough seas and the heavy surf made the landing a feat worthy of commemoration. Here again, according to Barros, the crews once more raised their complaints, and reluctantly Dias was at last obliged to turn for home. Afterwards the historians differed about the exact site of this Rio do Infante where Dias turned back, though most of them considered it to be the Great Fish River. But it was not here, at the ultimate point of his discoveries, that Dias raised his first *padrão*, either because the sea was too rough to permit his men to heave this half-ton piece of limestone out of the hold and land it safely on shore, or else because of the absence of a suitable site. But we know that at the earliest conjunction of suitable site and weather he raised a *padrão*. By the twentieth century it had vanished, and by the time I returned from two years of research in Portugal and other European countries in 1938 it had not been rediscovered. To find it was to become the object of my quest. Where did Dias raise his first and farthest cross?

V

The Farthest Cross of Bartolomeu Dias

BEFORE describing the discovery of the first and farthest *padrão* which Dias erected on the southern shores of Africa, it is necessary to turn to the early charts and chronicles in order to understand the difficulties involved in establishing the exact site, and the clues that eventually led me, at the very point of arriving back from my year of study in Portugal, to the solution of the mystery.

According to the account by Barros, which as we know was written half a century after the events he was describing, Dias and his men came to 'an islet which is in 32¾° south latitude, and here they placed the *padrão* named da Cruz, which name they gave to the islet, which is little more than a league from the mainland; and because there were two springs of water on it many called it the penedo das Fontes'; it was twenty-five leagues short of the Infante. Fernão Lopes de Castanheda, the contemporary of Barros, whose *História do descobrimento e conquista da India pelos Portugueses* is the most accurate of the chronicles in its references—unfortunately sparing to the predecessors of Vasco da Gama—tells us that Dias 'placed in certain spots some *padrões* which he took with him with crosses and the royal arms of Portugal. And the last was on an islet close to the mainland fifteen leagues behind the Rio do Infante, to which he gave the name ilhéu da Cruz'; elsewhere Catanheda says that the ilhéu da Cruz was five leagues short of the ilhéus Chãos (the present-day Bird Islands).

What is today known as St. Croix Island is in latitude 33° 48′ south, and it is just over a mile from the mainland; to add to the confusion, this, like the Rio do Infante, is another case where Dias duplicated names, for he called it ilhéu da Cruz to celebrate the *wooden* cross he raised there, and this led a number of historians to the erroneous conclusion that here also he erected his stone *padrão*. But St. Croix Island is a bare rock with no springs such as Barros described, and neither the guano collectors who frequented it nor deliberate searchers, like Dr. J. Hewitt of the Albany Museum at Grahamstown, had found the slightest trace of a stone column ever being erected there. Confusion became compounded when one considered the discrepancy between the distances given by Barros and Castanheda. Twenty-five leagues from St. Croix Island would take one ten miles east of the Great Fish River, while fifteen leagues from the same island would mean a spot roughly twenty-five miles west of that river. Castanheda's statement that the ilhéu da Cruz was five leagues short of the Bird Islands (without saying in which direction) was equally inapplicable to St. Croix Island, which is approximately eight leagues west of the Bird Islands.

From the chroniclers I turned to Pacheco Pereira, or rather to the late seventeenth-century transcriptions, with all their copyists' errors, which are the only versions that now survive of his *Esmeraldo de Situ Orbis*, prepared within a few years of the voyage of Dias. He described the Angra do Rico, which is undoubtedly the Angra do Roca of the early map-makers and the Algoa Bay of today. St. Croix Island, of course, lies in Algoa Bay, but Pacheco Pereira gives the following account of the island where the *padrão* was erected.

'Item. Five leagues beyond the Angra do Rico [i.e. Roca]

is an islet a little more than half a league from the land, which is called the Penedo das Fontes, which name Bartolomeu Dias gave it, who discovered this land by order of king Dom João—may he rest in peace—because he found there two springs of very good sweet water; and this rock is also called the ilhéu da Cruz, because the same Bartolomeu Dias placed there a stone *padrão*, a little taller than a man, with a cross on top. This *padrão* has three inscriptions, namely, one in Latin, one in Arabic, and the other in our Portuguese language. All three say the same thing, namely, that the king Dom João in the year of our lord Jesus Christ 1488 and so many years after the creation of the world, ordered this coast to be discovered by Bartolomeu Dias, captain of his vessels. This *padrão* can be seen from the sea when a man is close to the islet. Around it on the mainland are nothing but sand dunes, but the land adjacent to the shore beyond the sand dunes is very green; this land is low and well-wooded; and in places there are cultivated fields. Beyond this land along the coast are nothing but sand dunes, some large and some small. And this ilhéu da Cruz will be almost half a league in the sea. The coast from the Angra do Rico to here runs north-east by east and south-west by west and occupies five leagues of the route as we have said. And the said Penedo das Fontes is 33° 45′ from the equinoctial line towards the antarctic.'

Pacheco Pereira continues by remarking that it is twenty-five leagues from the ilhéu da Cruz to the Rio do Infante; between eight and ten leagues from the ilhéu da Cruz are the ilhéus Chãos (the Bird Islands); and from these it is fifteen leagues to the Infante.

This seemed to involve even greater confusion, for there was an obvious contradiction between the two parts of Pereira's statement. He begins by stating that the *padrão* was erected on an islet *beyond* Algoa Bay and therefore *east* of the Bird Islands, in a place where no island appeared on any of the maps with which I was familiar. On the other hand, by telling us that it is twenty-five leagues from the *padrão* to the Rio do Infante, and only fifteen leagues from the Bird Islands to the Infante, he seemed to indicate that the island on which the *padrão* was erected was ten leagues *west* of the Bird Islands, which brings one to the vicinity of St. Croix Island. Was Pacheco Pereira at this point falling into the same error as some modern authorities and confusing two different places both called ilhéu da Cruz? Certainly there were other unlikely points in his account, such as his reference to an Arabic inscription on the column, and the inconsistency between the two paragraphs of his description was obvious. Could the second have been added at some interval between the writing of the original and the preparation of the later transcription by a writer who, unlike Pereira, knew neither Dias nor Africa?

These doubts led me to re-examine the record by Álvaro Velho of Vasco da Gama's voyage; it was written nearer to the time of Dias's voyage than any other surviving document, and Vasco da Gama's chief pilot, Pero de Alenquer, had accompanied Dias. This confirmed unequivocally that Pacheco Pereira's first statement was correct, and that therefore the distances given later in the surviving versions of his rutter must be inaccurate, 'On Friday in the morning we had sight of land at what are called the ilhéus Chãos . . .,' said Álvaro Velho. 'From the ilhéus Chãos to the last *padrão* which Bartolomeu Dias placed is another five leagues; and from the *padrão* to the Rio do Infante it is fifteen leagues. Item. On the Saturday morning following we passed the last *padrão*.'

This left no doubt that the first *padrão* Dias erected, to

mark as closely as possible the end of his voyaging around
the extremity of Africa, must be sought not in Algoa Bay,
but to the east of it. At this moment I was actually following
the route which Dias had taken and looking out on the
shore which he had coasted, for I was returning home to
Durban in 1938 on one of the Union Castle mailboats after
my researches in Portugal. I had with me a photograph of
the portion of the Cantino map which showed southern
Africa, and I examined it closely with a magnifying glass.
It marked the Baía da Roca (or Algoa Bay), and the
ilhéus da Cruz were shown within the bay. To the east was
a headland, the Punta da Carrasqual, and beyond it the
Padõ de S. Greg(or)io; then came a Rio da Lagoa, and a
beach, and beyond that—as in the earlier part of Pacheco
Pereira's account—a Penedo das Fontes. But there was no
sign of the Rio do Infante. The Martellus map showed a
similar omission; its easternmost entry was 'ilha de Fonte'.
I began to wonder whether there was in fact any rock or
islet of the Fountains, or whether it was not all a confusion
with the name of Infante.

I finally turned to João de Lisboa and the rutter appended
to his 1514 *Livro de Marinharia*, and here my doubts were
resolved. João de Lisboa describes the route from Lisbon
to India. He tells of Cape Recife, at the entrance to Algoa
Bay, and he talks of the high ground in the interior that
reminds a Portuguese traveller of the Sintra hills. In the bay
itself he tells of the ilhéus da Cruz; one was larger than the
others, and it was possible to sail round this islet whatever
the wind, and at this point the bottom was clean. João de
Lisboa goes on to describe in some detail the sand dunes
along the shores of the bay, and the line of bush that is
visible behind them. He tells of the ilhéus Chãos (the Bird
Islands) and adds that one can pass between them and the

mainland in perfect safety because there is a depth of fifteen or sixteen fathoms (which agrees precisely with modern charts). East of the ilhéus Châos is a headland, the Ponta do Carrascal, covered with bush that resembles a grove of holm-oaks. At this point comes the decisive paragraph:

'Item. Know that from this point which is called the ponta do Carrascal about a league to the east there is on the shore an islet joined to the mainland and some sand dunes on the mainland covered with black bush; and this islet is not cut off from the sea. It is a knoll of rock which looks like an islet; and on this islet is the *padrão* which Bartolomeu Dias placed by order of the king Dom João— may he rest with God. And know that from the ilhéus Châos it is five leagues to where the *padrão* is situated.'

Was there in fact, five leagues or seventeen miles east of the Bird Islands, an islet that was not an islet but only looked like one, joined to the mainland by a stretch of low-lying beach and sand dune? The means of solving that difficulty lay close at hand. I left my cabin and made my way circumspectly through the First Class to the bridge of the mailboat. The officer of the watch was interested and sympathetic. He led me to the chart-room and took out the chart for the section of coast from Cape St. Francis to Waterloo Bay. And there, to my great excitement, I saw— marked on the coast eighteen miles from the Bird Islands— the legend 'False I. or Kwaai Hoek'. The officer turned up the appropriate volume of the *Africa Pilot*, and there I read: 'False Islet, or Kwaai hoek, is a dark-looking headland, 85 feet (25m9) high, which from seaward shows out against the white sand and resembles an islet. It is nearly perpendicular on its sea face and is connected to the mainland by sandy hillocks.' Obviously, it seemed to me in that euphoric moment, it was necessary only to go to False Islet and I would find the *padrão*.

Three miles west of False Islet, according to the chart, was Richmond Farm and the Bokness River. From there a road ran inland six miles to Alexandria village. Alexandria, I knew, was connected with Port Elizabeth by rail, and the ship would stop in Port Elizabeth for a whole day. The distance thence to Alexandria was only fifty-four miles, so I decided to catch a morning train to Alexandria and hire a taxi there to take me as close as possible to False Islet. But when I went ashore I found that though the train left at 9 a.m., it proceeded with such incredible slowness that it was not scheduled to arrive at Alexandria until 4 p.m., and was often late! There was only one chance, and that was to hire a taxi in Port Elizabeth. Two years in Europe on a scholarship of £20 a month, to cover travel, subsistence and all other expenses, had left little in my pocket, and to hire a taxi by the meter was impossible. However, on the advice of one of the drivers I went to the office and secured a price for a charter trip that made the journey possible, though the stewards would have to receive half the tip I had intended and I would have to depend on free transport to my home in Pietermaritzburg when I reached Durban.

We reached Alexandria, and ten miles beyond it the sea came into sight. We looked in vain for a track that might lead us close to the beach, and came eventually to the tiny village of Boesmansriviermond—Bushman's River Mouth. Among the thick bush that clothed the banks of the river there were some holiday shacks and the homes of a few retired people. We called at the store of Meneer Scheepers to ask for directions. False Islet meant nothing to him, but he knew the name Kwaaihoek, which means Angry Corner. We should return four miles up the road to a humble farm belonging to a coloured man called George Jacobs; if we drove across his land we could approach to within two miles of Kwaaihoek.

We went back and, leaving the taxi, I crossed a shallow valley that paralleled the coast and pushed my way for about two hundred yards through a tangle of bush, encountering a dangerous-looking snake on the way. I emerged on the top of a sand dune at least a hundred feet high. Before me stretched a mile of dune and beach, golden and almost blinding in the brilliant sunlight after the darkness of the bush. Beyond rose a black-topped knoll, the crest of Kwaaihoek. A quarter of a mile to the left stood another dark hillock, but lower and less prominent, and still farther on yet another; but the knoll before me was the most conspicuous, and as it was the westernmost of the three projections, a *padrão* placed there would be seen first by the look-outs of vessels proceeding from Europe towards Asia. This surely was the site that Dias chose.

On the top of the knoll, however, I found nothing but a modern concrete survey beacon. But, as I reflected, the *padrão* had already disappeared from view by 1576, when Mesquita Perestrêlo surveyed the coast; moreover, there was no guarantee that the present highest point of the knoll was the highest point in 1488, and in any case it was covered with scrub, two or three feet high, that would have concealed a fallen column. I scuffled around in the scrub, but found nothing of interest except the fact that it was growing in deep sand into which any heavy object would have sunk down. I returned to the taxi disappointed not to have found any trace of the *padrão*, but the appearance of the place accurately matched the description given by João de Lisboa, and I was convinced that this was indeed the site where Dias raised the monument that celebrated the end of his voyage.

At Durban my brother met me; he was then a lecturer in economics at the Pietermaritzburg Technical College, and as he was on vacation he offered, as soon as he had heard my story, to drive me to Kwaaihoek so that I might continue my investigation there. His car had passed its prime, and in the 1930s the national road that was to link Natal and the Cape was little more than a dream in blueprint, but after several days of travel I was back at Jacobs' farm. There we found a way through the bush and set up a camp just within its shelter, on the edge of the dunes. We feared that fresh water might be difficult to find, but Jacobs led us down the sand dune to the hollow at its foot, and there, within a foot of the surface, was an much fresh water as we needed. It was doubtless such waterholes, opened by Bushmen—and in our investigations we found a considerable number of late stone-age implements—that led to this spot being named the Penedo das Fontes.

We had driven from Durban to Kwaaihoek through unceasing rain, but on the night of our arrival the rain stopped and the wind started or, more correctly, resumed. Kwaaihoek lies in one of the windiest corners of South Africa, and we were there in January, the windiest month of the year. We crossed the waste of dunes to the knoll through a cloud of sand reminiscent of the Sahara but perhaps even more formidable, for the rain had weighted each particle so that they flew through the air like shot. The surveyor's beacon creaked and shuddered in the blast, the low bushes pressed close to the ground, the sea boiled against the foot of the cliff, and we knew at once why the local fishermen called this Angry Corner.

We had brought a steel rod, five feet long and sharpened at one end, to probe the sandy stratum at the crest of the knoll. We stretched a cord east and west past the surveyor's beacon to serve as a base line and we hammered in the steel probe at intervals of three feet along that line, working from the beacon eastwards. Six times the steel went in to its full length. The seventh time it went in three feet and then jarred on something solid. The eighth time it went in two feet, the ninth time three feet and the tenth time three feet. On the eleventh it again penetrated to its full length, and so it did on the twelfth and the thirteenth. In an area some nine feet across the probe encountered what must obviously be a large solid object.

We cut away a patch of scrub and began to dig. Soon we started finding rocks, the largest of which required our combined efforts to shift. They were all made of the soft dune-rock of which the cliff and the base of the knoll were composed, until my brother excitedly drew my attention to a piece he had just uncovered. It was quite unlike the rest—not yellowish-brown, but pinkish-white; not rough in texture and soft, but hard, crystalline and smooth, looking for all the world like marble. We cleared the sand away from it, and looked down on a straight, level face. In fact, when we lifted it we found that it had two level faces parallel to each other; they were eight and a half inches apart, while the stone was about a foot long and four inches deep. It was most certainly not a local rock.

During the next few minutes we dug out two more fragments of the same stone, one of them also eight and a half inches across. Then we found a piece with six level faces; it was a rectangular block, four and a quarter inches across, which ended in a bevelled face, 45° from the perpendicular. It was not as crystalline as the other fragments, but obviously it had been worked by hand; it could conceivably be the top arm of the cross that had crowned the *padrão*.

By now a growing pile of sand and rocks ringed the hole

we had dug, and an almost spherical rock, which we had placed on the seaward side of the mound, rolled away, gathering momentum down a steep slope where the wind had thinned the scrub, and plunged over the edge of the cliff. It marked the cliff in its fall, and looking down we saw that it had entered the water at a place where there was a kind of recess in the cliff. Off shore there were several large rocks, one looking like a caravel, another like a submarine, but this grotesque fleet failed to lessen the force of the surf which broke against the foot of the cliff and threw spray almost into our faces. If that lump of dune stone could fall thus from the crest of the knoll into the sea, could not the same thing have happened to the fragments of a shattered *padrão*?

That afternoon the wind began to fall, and at sundown the moon rose in a clear sky. Early next morning we were off to take advantage of better weather and a spring tide. On the western side of the knoll there was deep water, and the only way of reaching the place where the rock had fallen was from the Bushman's River side. We scrambled down a steep bank whose sides were honeycombed by the nesting holes of kingfishers to a cove that might have been transplanted from the west of England. We crossed the rock spur that protected the cove and climbed down into a tangle of great rocks. The tide was still high and we had to wait, but it ebbed rapidly and then we were at the foot of the cliff, searching among the rocks for the recess we had seen from above.

We found it, and my brother looked into a pool and called me over. At the bottom of the water lay an object, covered in oysters and mussels, and masked by strands of seaweed at each returning wave, that looked as though it had a rectangular face. We stripped away the weed, and in a few minutes the tide had receded far enough for the pool to remain undisturbed. The stone we had seen was about two and a half feet long and it had three level faces; the top face was about eight and a half inches across. But it was so encrusted with marine growths that we could not determine the nature of the rock until we took an axe and chipped off a corner; it was the same kind of crystalline stone as the pieces we had found on the crest of the knoll. The *padrão* had obviously been shattered and this was part of its column.

With a billy-can and tin mugs we emptied the pool. Being harder than the surrounding rocks, the block—assisted by the wash and scour of the sea—had scooped a bed for itself so that half its depth was submerged. We wedged it free and hoisted it up; tying a rope to each end, we raised it from the pool and started carrying it round the bottom of the cliff; no easy task, for we had to cross rocks between six and ten feet high, and the block seemed heavier with each yard we dragged and pushed and lifted it. (Later we learnt that it weighed 177 pounds, but there were times when it seemed far heavier!) The tide turned, and came rushing in with unexpected vigour, so that we were soon up to our waists in water. Between waves we worked the block forward a few more feet, and as each breaker came surging in we protected it as best we could. There were times when we feared we would have to abandon it, but there was no snug pool where it could be left, and we struggled on, raising it finally—and certainly none too soon—on to the shingle above the tidemark at the head of the cove.

The next day we devoted to transporting the block over a mile of sand dunes, in which operation the farmer George Jacobs with his donkey-sledge came to our assistance. The three of us carried the block to the lee of the knoll, wrapped it in sacking, and tied it to the sledge. In a zigzag erratic progress, we made our way along the valleys between the dunes. Every now and again, the donkeys would become separated from the sledge, and just as often one part of the sledge would separate itself from the rest. But Jacobs was resourceful, and for every crisis he would produce a sufficient length of wire, but even his ingenuity was defeated by the last 100-foot dune. The donkeys plodded up, reached a third of the way to the top, and then the dune poured them back to the bottom. Next time they rushed it, and got halfway up, but then, though their legs went like pistons, they made only one foot for every two they lost. In the end, after incredible efforts on our part, in which we seemed to be carrying donkeys and sledge as well as the well-bewired block, we reached the top, and outside our tent the sledge disintegrated irremediably.

The next morning, after a curious and inoffensive buck snuffling around our tent had set us on nervous guard, we reconstructed the sledge, pushed it to our car, loaded the block, and struck camp. It was obvious the car would not long endure that added load, so in Alexandria we searched out the local undertaker, who made a coffin for the block in which it fitted as snugly as it had done in its seaweed rockpool. Since by now we could not afford to send it quickly by passenger train, we dispatched it, carriage forward, by goods train.

Meanwhile, the problems of authentication had already begun to haunt my mind. If these fragments of rock, allegedly from the final Dias *padrão*, and found near the mouth of Bushman's River in the Cape Province, made their first appearance in my native Natal, who would believe our accounts of their provenance? I had not heard of the widened powers that had been given to the Historical Monuments Commission in 1934, and therefore I did not take what afterwards I realized would have been the appropriate course: to request the Magistrate of Alexandria to keep them in custody until the Commission had decided what should be done with them. Instead—with what later was revealed to be ill-judged rashness—I telephoned the *Eastern Province Herald* in Port Elizabeth, and the next day the newspaper carried a front-page story; headed:

REMARKABLE FIND AT BUSHMAN'S RIVER
Cross said to have been erected by Bartholomew Dias in 1488
NATAL MAN'S DISCOVERY
After Perusal of Charts in Portugal

In the meantime, driving eastward to Natal, I was out of touch with the rest of the world, and I was therefore somewhat surprised on returning to Pietermaritzburg to find an ominously official letter awaiting me. It was from Professor C. van Riet Lowe, Secretary of the Commission for the Preservation of Natural and Historical Monuments, Relics and Antiques, and it enclosed the copy of a telegram he had sent to the magistrate in Alexandria ordering that 'ALL FOSSICKING OR IRRESPONSIBLE DIGGING BE STOPPED UNTIL AXELSONS EXAMINATION COMPLETED . . . PLEASE REPORT ALL DETAILS OF DISCOVERY TO THIS OFFICE IMMEDIATELY.' In a covering letter, he told the Magistrate that I was 'recognized as an expert by the Commission and should be given every facility to continue his investigations provided he is made to realize that the ultimate destination of every portion of the cross is a matter that must be referred to this Commission, and that no dispersal of fragments must under any circumstances be permitted'. He asked that if I were still in the district I should be asked to communicate

128

1 Kwaaihoek, showing the site, before the final excavation, of the stone cross raised by Bartolomeu Dias in 1488

The site of the stone cross raised by Bartolomeu Dias near Lüderitz, 1488

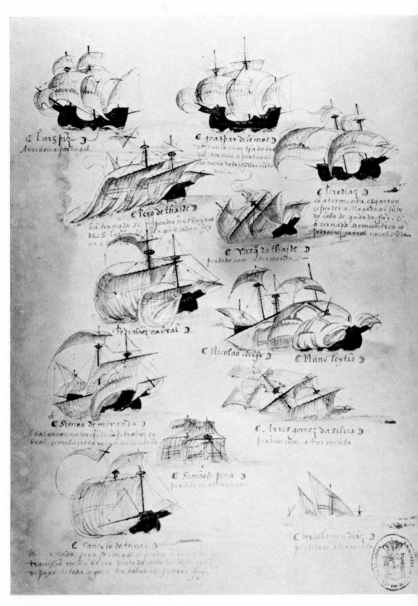

x Cabral's fleet, 1500, and the sinking in the south Atlantic of Bartolomeu Dias
caravel

with the Commission immediately, but all the bewildered Justice at Alexandria could do was to telegraph in reply 'PLEASE ADVISE AXELSON HAVE COURTESY INTRODUCE HIMSELF LOCAL MAGISTRATE OTHERWISE IMPOSSIBLE MY GUARDS DIFFERENTIATE UNAUTHORISED AND AUTHORISED OPERATIONS.'

It was obvious that I had inadvertently stirred an archaeological hornet's nest, and, after telegraphing the Magistrate that all operations at Kwaaihoek until I returned from Pietermaritzburg were unauthorized, I reported to the Historical Monuments Commission and informed them that I had already submitted the smaller fragments which I had brought with me by car to Dr. L. C. King, the geologist at Natal University College. In my report I remarked that, while it would be an extraordinary coincidence if relics found from tracing documentary evidence in Portugal were not in fact parts of the *padrão*, certainty would be impossible without a comparative observation of the limestone found at Kwaaihoek and that which outcrops near Lisbon.

An encouraging answer came from Professor van Riet Lowe of the Historical Monuments Commission, and an equally encouraging letter from Professor Fouché who had originally started me on my search, but shortly afterwards I was disappointed to receive a report from Dr. King in which he expressed the opinion that the fragments brought by road appeared to be of limestone from the local Alexandria beds close to Kwaaihoek, and that, since natural parallel jointing in limestone is not uncommon, the appearance of the surfaces having been sawed was not conclusive evidence that they were in fact worked by man, though they appeared to have been transported to the spot by artificial means. Later, however, when he had seen the large piece sent by rail, Dr. King confirmed that here indeed was evidence of

c c—I

human workmanship, and that, though the 'nature of the rock, a coastal limestone containing fossil shells (including probable Oysters), is such that it unfortunately compares rather readily with some of the beds of the nearby-situated Alexandria Series', he acknowledged the probability that such coastal limestone could also exist 'in the neighbourhood of Lisbon where Dias's cross was made' and stressed the need to secure suitable specimens from both Alexandria and Lisbon for comparison.

Meanwhile there had been activity, both disquieting and encouraging, in other directions. The Magistrate in Alexandria sent me a very formal letter telling me that every fragment of the alleged cross must be disposed as instructed by the Historical Monuments Commission, and that these were the instructions he had received 'but obviously I could not act as you had left my District before I knew anything about the matter.' He informed me that he had put Jacobs in charge of the site and that he had satisfied himself there had been no interference. He further enclosed an extract from Act 4 of 1934, Section 9 (2): 'No person shall, without the written consent of the Commission, destroy or damage any monument or relic or make any alteration thereto by removing it from its original site.' It was clear that if the relics were not in fact authentic, there had been a great stir over nothing, but if they were, then I had committed an offence in the eyes of the law.

To compensate for this disturbing situation, Professor Fouché travelled the 350 miles from Johannesburg to look at the block of limestone and the other fragments, and after examining them he said: 'I have been on my knees before a true cross.' Not only did he thus give an historian's support to my as yet unproved discovery, but he also persuaded the University of Witwatersrand to finance further investigations at Kwaaihoek on condition that I go there as soon as possible. Today the grant of £40 for travel expenses and equipment, £20 a month for maintenance and £15 for native labour, seems very modest, but in 1938 it was generous. Professor van Riet Lowe of the Historical Commission had been won over, and I spent a few days learning the elements of scientific excavation from him before I set out with his blessing.

This time I went by train to Port Elizabeth, where I bought such necessary equipment as picks and shovels, screening and rope, and then caught the 9 a.m. train to Alexandria. It proved as leisurely a journey as I had been promised when I first arrived in Port Elizabeth. The train consisted of a dozen goods trucks and one passenger coach. At each station and each halt the diminutive engine would shunt trucks away and add different trucks, and it was after 5 p.m. that the fifty-four-mile journey was completed and the train reached Alexandria. My first act was to call on the Magistrate, Mr. N. B. Arbuthnot, who proved not only friendly, but also hospitable. He invited me to be his guest for the night, and at dinner he and his wife told me of the interest that had built up in the district because of my search. Two great questions troubled local minds. The first was how much gold I had already found. The second was how much more I still hoped to dig up.

The next day Mr. Arbuthnot drove me as near to Kwaaihoek as a car could reach, and I set up camp. The previous camp site had been too distant, but it was a problem to find a place relatively sheltered from the incessant wind, and when I did finally secure one by levelling a platform on the side of the dune towards Bushman's River, the sandslides were so frequent that sometimes my tent had to be dug out twice in a single day. As for the tent itself which

I had hired in Port Elizabeth, this turned out to be more like a mosquito net—which was certainly not needed—than a structure meant to give shelter, for it kept out neither the rain nor the sand.

George Jacobs was persuaded to head the digging team, and he recruited a friend, Isaac, and several other assistants. We cleared the top of the knoll of scrub, and I laid out with string a grid with five-foot squares. We started digging down, square by square, a foot at a time. We removed numbers of boulders, and every shovel of sand we sieved through quarter-inch screening. Almost at once we began to find pieces of the limestone, which I immediately recognized. Each piece was marked with its exact location on the grid, and its depth from a datum point on the surface. We tied labels to the larger pieces; the smaller pieces we placed in envelopes and quickly exhausted the supply of these at Meneer Scheepers's store.

It was while we were in the midst of this work that a crucial letter arrived from Professor Fouché. He had submitted the already excavated fragments of the cross to Dr. Haughton, the Director of the Geological Survey, who had personally worked on the Alexandria beds. Haughton had not only declared that the limestone had undoubtedly been worked by human hand; he had also confirmed that it was most definitely not local rock. He now proposed to examine the fossil structure of the stone and to compare this with information provided by Portuguese geological publications.

In the process of his examination Haughton had actually established that two of the smaller fragments fitted into the larger block, and, as Professor Fouché concluded, 'This makes it all the more necessary for you to find *further* bits, since we now have only *two* separate, or rather *different* bits:

the big block (in three parts) and the largest of the small ones. Go to it!'

I was finding 'further bits' in abundance, but the inhabitants of Bushman's River Mouth seemed intent on casting doubt on the authenticity of the discoveries. One of the villagers told me that I was wasting my time digging up the gravestone of a shipwrecked Lascar seaman whose body had been washed ashore in 1918 and had been buried at Kwaaihoek; only after lengthy inquiries did I find a man who had actually helped to bury the Lascar, and he reassured me that the grave had actually been dug halfway between Kwaaihoek and Bushman's River, and nothing had been placed on it but a pile of stones. A few evenings later I went to the village again, and a woman told me that fifty years ago the oldest inhabitant of Bushman's River had built a summer cottage on the crest of Kwaaihoek; it was common knowledge in the neighbourhood, she asserted, that I was finding fragments of the pillars he had built to support the roof of his verandah. I went to see the oldest inhabitant at his farm five or six miles up the river, cutting across country through the bush. The old man remembered the cottage perfectly well. 'Did it have a verandah?' I asked him. 'Yes, of course it had a stoep. Where else can you sit and drink and look at the view and think great thoughts?' 'Were there pillars to the verandah?' 'Of course there were pillars!' he answered rather testily. 'I had to have a roof over the stoep to keep the sun off. How could the roof keep up without pillars?' And then, perhaps regretting his abruptness, he offered to point out the site of his cottage. The next day, despite his considerable age, he rode on horseback to Kwaaihoek. As soon as he reached the knoll he dismounted. 'Who on earth would want to build a cottage here?' he exclaimed. 'Far too windy—and no water up here. No, mine was much better situated.' And he pointed towards the Bokness River, to a site as far west of Kwaaihoek as the Lascar's grave had been to the east. 'And I don't know why you're getting so excited about my pillars,' he added. 'You'll never find them now. They were made of wood and they'll have rotted away long ago.'

We kept on working, and the fragments of limestone kept on turning up until eventually we found eight fragments which seemed to settle finally the question of authenticity, for they contained the remains of an inscription and fitted together. I sent them at once to Professor Fouché. 'There is indubitable lettering', he answered immediately, 'and Gothic at that, on those bits, such as one would expect of XVth century Portuguese.'

The largest fragments of the *padrão* were within two feet of the surface. Three feet down there was a marked thinning of even the smaller pieces, below four feet there were hardly any fragments at all, and none at a depth of more than five feet. But the rules of archaeology demand that one go down to rock bottom when possible, and this we did in the area below the main concentration of local boulders and limestone fragments. We reached a depth of nineteen and a half feet before we eventually struck the bedrock of tufa. We had removed and screened more than twenty tons of sand, and in all we had found no less than 5,000 pieces of limestone, but most of them were minute.

Apart from the limestone we made some interesting finds: pieces of heavily rusted iron, slivers of lead, a fragment of glass, and some charcoal, though the last did not offer the kind of vital clue it would have provided in the modern age of carbon-14 dating. The iron looked like the corroded remnants of nails, which the Portuguese may have brought ashore to present to the local Africans, or which may have held together a timber casing for the cross. The charcoal may well have been the remnants of driftwood brought up to make a fire on which the lead could be melted. When Vasco da Gama, on his return voyage, landed on an island near Moçambique to raise a *padrão*, Álvaro Velho records that 'So heavy was a shower of rain that we were not able to make fire with which to melt lead to fix the cross, so the *padrão* remained without it.' Dias and his men were evidently more fortunate with the weather and succeeded in melting their lead. As for the fragment of glass, this was obviously from an old hand-blown bottle; it doubtless contained sacramental wine, for it is likely that mass was said (as Álvaro Velho tells us it was when Vasco da Gama raised the *padrão* off Moçambique) when the cross at Kwaaihoek was dedicated to São Gregorio.

The hole we had dug extended to the cliff on the seaward face of the knoll, and we did not neglect the cliff itself. We searched the broad ledge at the top, and, dangling on the end of a rope, I examined the ledges as far down as water level. It was obvious that large pieces of the cliff face had broken away and plunged into the sea comparatively recently, and there might be more fragments of the *padrão* lying beneath them. At low tide, particularly in the periods of new and full moon, we therefore attacked the lumps of soft rock with axes, sledge-hammers and wedges, and as soon as we had reduced them to manageable size we levered and rolled them out of the area we wanted to search. We also removed deposits of marine worms, in some places more than three feet thick, and under these deposits we found two more fragments of limestone buried in the sand; the largest was the familiar eight and a half inches across and nearly a foot long.

It still seemed possible that the sea itself, beyond low

water mark, might contain more fragments. Beyond the knoll there were two large rocks which projected seaward and converged in such a manner that their tips were only thirty feet apart, and at a low spring tide we filled fifty sandbags and tried to build a dam, but the sea was too strong for us. A fortnight later we tried again with two hundred bags, and this kept the sea away while we made good progress and cleared a large area down to rock bottom. Then a breeze sprang up from the south-west and the waves washed over our wall. One of my assistants, a member of a nearby mission church, volunteered to pray that the next day the wind blow from the north-east. His prayers were all too successful, for the wind blew in the specified direction, but at gale force, so that the seas washed over the rocks, the dam and everything else, and buried the area in a great drift of sand. Nevertheless, these strenuous operations had been well worth while, for we recovered from them an important fragment of the cross, 19 inches long by the usual $8\frac{1}{2}$ inches across, and 4 inches deep.

It was during the last phase of my work at Kwaaihoek that I received from Portugal a letter which revealed to me that other scholars had already drawn from the maps and chronicles very similar conclusions to my own regarding the actual location of the farthermost *padrão* erected by Bartolomeu Dias, and that it was only in the discovery of the solid material evidence that I could claim originality. The letter was from Captain A. Fontoura da Costa, who congratulated me on my find, and drew my attention to a paper which he had published in 1935 in the yearbook of the Club Militar Naval at Lisbon; in this admirable essay, with which I was then unfamiliar, he had identified the site of Dias's easternmost *padrão* as False Island, and he told me in his letter that in a paper which still remained unpublished

Admiral Ernesto de Vasconcelos had come to the same conclusion. Years later, I was to find that we had all been anticipated in an article that appeared in 1921 in the *Journal of the South African Association for the Advancement of Science*. My discovery, in other words, merely made certain a possibility that had already occurred to other students of the history of Portuguese exploration.

It was on the 31st March that I made my last defeated effort to hold back the sea. By this time the recovery of fragments on the crest of Kwaaihoek had also come to an end, and I returned to Johannesburg, where Professor van Riet Lowe began the task of fitting the largest pieces together in a sand bath and I carefully plotted out on paper the locations of all the finds: the boulders of local stone, the fragments of limestone, the pieces of iron, lead, charcoal and glass. From this plan it became evident that the *padrão* had been erected some twenty-two feet to the east of the surveyor's beacon.

Then, at the end of June, there came a letter from Magistrate Arbuthnot in Alexandria which suggested that my search had not been complete. The caprice of the seas had apparently washed out a part of the pool where I had experienced defeat, and there, in a spot which I had not investigated, George Jacobs 'has spotted an object which interests him greatly but with commendable scientific rectitude he refuses to commit himself until he has had an opportunity of applying his scientific knowledge (or crowbar) thereto. Through rubbing shoulders with you the old boy has assimilated some of your reticence in these matters! He says the surge of the tide will not permit access to it and he does not hope for any quietening of the tides until about September, and until he can "chip" it he cannot be certain. He says it is about two feet long and in appearance has the same angles and other outward appearances as the others . . . He says one end of this object looks suspiciously as if it would fit the base of one of the other blocks. There are also other much smaller stray pieces lying around it. He is going to watch the seas in case he can get nearer it but is dubious of any success without outside help.'

It was impossible for me to return to Kwaaihoek, since I had just started teaching in Natal. Professor Fouché was disturbed about the report, since he feared that in my absence there might be come 'irresponsible or unauthorized fossicking', but he thought that if the Magistrate 'can, and will, assume some sort of directing authority and let Jacobs work under him, perhaps they could carry on'. The Magistrate did indeed take matters in hand, and imagined that he was directing George Jacobs, who on his side gave no more information than he wished, since he had no intention of failing to reap the credit for the discovery of what he rightly suspected might be a most important section of the *padrão*. The comedy that was played out, certainly unknown to the Magistrate, was revealed to me by the letters that followed the successful recovery of the fragment on the 22nd September. Magistrate Arbuthnot wired the news to Professor Fouché, and followed up his telegram with a letter in which he remarked that the measurements of the piece recovered were 18 inches by $8\frac{1}{4}$ inches by 6 inches.

'The story of its recovery is a somewhat long one and will do for another time. Suffice it to say that I had instructed the Coloured man Jacobs to start making daily attempts from yesterday and we would join him today. He tried with assistance yesterday but the attempt had to be abandoned. This morning I took with me Messrs. Colesky, Phillipson and Scheepers and we commenced operations at Kwaaihoek at 8 a.m. Equinox is tomorrow but the Port Captain [of Port Elizabeth] advised trying the day before also. We had wonderful luck with the weather, it being the quietest dawn I have known for many a long month. At first Jacobs failed to locate it, and it was just before the incoming tide commenced being troublesome that he rediscovered it. A huge rock had to be bodily lifted by ten men before operations leading to its recovery could be commenced.'

Jacobs, who also wrote to me, had a significantly different tale to tell:

'You will undoubtedly be anxious to know where I found the stone. It is about five yards beyond the spot where you and your brother found the very first piece.

'I do hope that you always find a place for me in a corner of your memory.

'When the magistrate asked me to mark the spot on the snapshot with a pin I purposely made the mark in the wrong place because at that moment I did not know who was going to be present on the 22nd Sept., and somebody else may claim the honour of having found the stone. If you still remember, you once warned me that the Europeans were jealous of me and I therefore took no chances.

'On the 22nd I stood on the spot from the very minute I got in the water, whilst I directed the gentlemen to dive at a spot a few yards beyond. I found it very amusing to see the expert divers dive for something which they would never find.

'When I saw the tide was beginning to come in I started to feel about in the water. This aroused suspicion and all the people crowded round me. I then lifted the stone out of the water. Isaac helped me to do it.'

In this way, George Jacobs made sure that he and his friend Isaac gained the credit that was undoubtedly their due for the great part they had played in the discovery of the monument Dias raised. For my part, I was greatly encouraged by the letter I received from Magistrate Arbuthnot. 'It is far more symmetrical and uninjured than any of the previous fragments,' he told me in describing the salvaged stone. 'It has not a vestige of seagrowth, showing that it has always been embedded in sand, the best preservative. When it came out of the water, it was a picture of sparkling red-streaked marble. Strange, though, how it dulls right off almost immediately after being exposed to light.'

When it was finally assembled, with all the fragments fitted together as exactly as possible, the *padrão* was almost complete in its original form, and this was so disconcertingly different from that of the *padrões* erected by Cão as to arouse a momentary incredulity, particularly among scholars in Portugal. For it was a simple square column surmounted by a cross without the intervening square block containing the arms of Portugal which had been part of Cão's *padrões*; it also differed considerably, as we shall see, from the sketch made by Captain Thompson, R.N., in the eighteenth century which is our only record of the actual appearance of the *padrão* that Dias raised some months later on his return journey at Lüderitz.

Nevertheless, the *padrão* was eventually accepted as genuine—though one Portuguese historian continued to insist that the fragments with inscription had been inserted upside-down, whilst by inverting them he could read the letters TS, perhaps OM/DCLA/MPA/BN(?) N(?)—and there followed a series of disputes by local patriots as to where the monument should be preserved. The people of Bushman's River Mouth, despite their early scepticism, now assumed that the *padrão* would be re-erected on its original site. The Alexandria Divisional Council argued that its safety demanded it be kept in the nearest town, Alexandria. Rhodes University and the Albany Museum contended that, as the nearest academic and cultural centre, Grahamstown provided the most appropriate setting, while Port Elizabeth put in its claim as the nearest city. Naturally, the Portuguese were also interested, and the Johannesburg *Daily Express* published a characteristically sensational story which reported that 'A diplomatic war between Portugal and South Africa is being fought over the ownership of the 500-year old Bartholomew Dias Cross.'

The Historical Monuments Commission finally settled these complex claims by entrusting the monument to the University of Witwatersrand, and by making concrete replicas to be sent to the two places with the strongest claims, Portugal and Kwaaihoek. In August 1939, the Portuguese Minister of Colonies, Dr. Francisco Vieira Machado, travelled to Johannesburg to unveil the re-constructed original, and in 1941, the Governor-General of South Africa, Sir Patrick Duncan, accompanied by members of the diplomatic corps travelling by ox wagon over the dunes, unveiled the replica at Kwaaihoek.

The establishment of the exact spot where Dias erected his first *padrão* necessarily re-opened the question of the identity of the Rio do Infante, the farthest point of the explorer's journey, where he turned homeward for Europe.

Up to this point, as I have said, it had generally been assumed that the Rio do Infante was identical with the Great Fish River, the next stream of any importance to enter the sea east of Bushman's River. Now, however, a farther river, the Keiskama, appeared a possibility.

On the location of the Rio do Infante the early maps are unhelpful. The Florentine Martellus map marks the *padrão*, and the Ilha da Fonte, which may be a garbled reference either to the Penedo das Fontes, or to the Rio do Infante, for immediately beyond appears the estuary of an unnamed river. The Cantino map in Modena marks, in turn, the *padrão*, the Rio da Lagoa, the Praia das Alagoas, the Penedo das Fontes, Furna (a hollow), and the Rio do Infante; some of these names are impossible to identify, the placing of the *padrão* in relation to the Penedo das Fontes is incorrect, and it is impossible to determine where on the coastline as at present known the Rio do Infante would lie. The river figures in a third map somewhat later than either the Cantino or the Martellus chart. Drawn about 1506, probably by a Portuguese, this appears in F. Kunstmann's *Atlas zur Entdeckungsgeschichte* (and is commonly known as Kunstmann III); it shows the *padrão*, the Penedo das Fontes, and then an extremely broad Rio do Infante, at which point the map ends. There is, of course, no such prominent river so close to the *padrão* as this map suggests.

As for the chroniclers, the only one who is completely clear in his description is Álvaro Velho, who personally visited the coast less than ten years after Dias. He unequivocally states that it was fifteen leagues from the *padrão* to the Rio do Infante, and this distance would have taken the expedition exactly to the mouth, not of the Great Fish River, but of the Keiskama River. This river has a narrow mouth, but within it broadens into a wide basin, and this may be partly responsible for the representation in the Kunstmann map.

The confusion in Pacheco Pereira's *Esmeraldo de Situ Orbis* regarding the site of the *padrão* extends also to that of the Rio do Infante. When he mistakes St. Croix Island for the island of the *padrão*, and says it is twenty-five leagues to the Rio do Infante, he takes us to within a few miles of the Keiskama. But when in another place he says it is fifteen leagues from the Bird Islands to the Infante, he takes us only a little way beyond the Great Fish River. It is both exasperating and tantalizing that the only surviving copies of the *Esmeraldo de Situ Orbis* both break off at the words 'Jaz ho Rio do Infante . . .' ('The Rio do Infante lies . . .').

The sixteenth-century chronicler João de Lisboa is equally ambivalent; he declares that it is ten leagues from the *padrão* to the Infante, a distance that would have taken Dias approximately to the Great Fish River. At the same time his very detailed description of the intervening country would seem to cover a stretch of more than ten leagues, while his reference to extensive sand dunes and many waterways before the Rio do Infante itself is an accurate description of the country bordering the Keiskama to the south-west.

Taking into account João de Lisboa's description of the country and Álvaro Velho's estimate of the distance from the *padrão* at Kwaaihoek to the Rio do Infante, it would seem that the mouth of the Keiskama River at Hamburg, about thirty miles south-west of East London, is the farthest point reached by Bartolomeu Dias before he turned westward to explore the coastline which he had missed by sailing too far to the south.

Postscript

Professor Vernon Forbes, authority especially on eighteenth-century travellers in South Africa, has recently been examining photostat copies of the journals and field-books (discovered in England in 1964) of Colonel R. J. Gordon, military commander of the Cape under the Netherlands East India Company, who made a number of notable journeys. On the 13th February 1786 'two hours on foot

W.S.W. of the Bushmans River mouth' he reached the mouth of the Bokna, i.e. Bokness, river, where he set up equipment to take celestial observations. He then 'went E.N.E. along the shore that is sandy here, to a prominent green hill on which I found a shattered-to-pieces old monument. Collected the fragments together in order to take them in the waggon to the Cape.' Professor Forbes comments, 'Gordon gives no indication whether he realized the nature and significance of the monument. But the facts that he made it the terminal point of his journey and recorded his decision to take what fragments of it that he could find back to Cape Town, surely argue that he had more than an inkling of its probable importance. Presumably he removed all the inscribed fragments that he could because these offered a means of ascertaining by whom, when and why the monument had been erected. His journal does not state whether he carried out his intention of loading the pieces on his waggon and transporting them to Cape Town. But it would be inconsistent with what is known of his character had he failed to carry out his intention, and there seems little reason to doubt that the pieces of the *padrão* that he had collected reached Cape Town.' Safely arrived in Cape Town he would probably have taken the remains to his headquarters; but Professor Forbes has found no fragments of the distinctive limestone at the Castle and the house where Gordon lived has been recently demolished.

VI

The Homeward Journey of Bartolomeu Dias

It was on the 12th March 1488 that Bartolomeu Dias raised his farthest *padrão*, and then resumed his homeward journey, with much regret and—according to the chronicler Barros— as if the cross he left on its lonely rock were a son sentenced to irrevocable banishment. He was sad too that, having come so far, and achieved so much, he had still not found his way to the Arabian Sea.

There is little in the chronicles regarding the homeward voyage, even though west of the Cape of Good Hope and some way north along the west coast of Africa, Dias was in fact discovering a coastline unknown to European voyagers. To reconstruct his movements we have to rely partly on the hardly more abundant references of the early maps, and partly on what we know of other early Portuguese voyages in this region.

It is likely that as far as Mossel Bay, where they already knew the coast, the caravels put out to sea where the pilots would have discovered the westward-flowing current some miles off shore. But beyond Cape Vacca it was an unfamiliar shore, and Dias must have followed it as closely as rocks and weather would allow. The rocky beaches soon gave way to sand, and the long expanse of Still Bay beach came into view—the Terra de São João of the early maps. The mountains of the Langeberg reared their blue crests in the distant background as the ships sailed into the broad deep bay which Dias called Shelter Bay. Into it flowed a river, the estuary of which a later Portuguese captain, Manuel de Mesquita Perestrêlo, who came here in 1575–6 to survey the coast and find harbours where ships might be repaired and replenished, described as being large enough to shelter the largest armada from all winds. Nevertheless, because of the heavy surf and the strong easterly winds blowing at the time Perestrêlo could not cross the bar, and had to land in a cove close to Cape Infanta—a name which again commemorates the adventurous captain of the *São Pantaleão*—and from there his party had to go overland to survey the wide and deep river flowing into the bay, the Breë River of today which Dias called the Nazaré.

The first point on this homeward journey for which it seems possible to establish a date is Struys Bay, since on the Cantino map this is named Aguada de San Jorgy, and this suggests that Dias anchored here on St. George's Day, or 23rd April. This means that he took six weeks to sail the comparatively short distance of 345 miles from Kwaaihoek, which at first sight seems surprising, since the crews and the commanders alike would by this time be anxious to rejoin the storeship as quickly as possible. However, it must be remembered that in March and April sailing ships proceeding from the east towards the Cape of Good Hope are likely to encounter adverse weather conditions, for the wind in this season blows more often from the north-west than the east. It is also possible that the caravels lost company or that one or both of them suffered damage in a gale and had to make repairs; the latter possibility is reinforced by the fact that they named the nearby point after St. Brendan, the navigator monk of Ireland who is said to have discovered strange lands in the Atlantic during the Middle Ages, and Brendan's Day is celebrated on the 16th May, which means that the ships must have stayed for at least three weeks in Struys Bay, being put into shape for the northward voyage and perhaps renewing their supplies of fresh food for the weeks of sailing that still separated them from the store-ship.

The Cabo de São Brandão was renamed by later Portuguese voyagers the Cabo das Agulhas, and Cape Agulhas it has remained. This means the Cape of the Compass Needles, and it received the name because there was no magnetic variation at this point at that time; a compass needle pointed due north. If they stayed so long in Struys Bay, Dias and his pilots cannot have failed to observe this phenomenon, but they appear to have been unaware of the fact that when they left Struys Bay and sailed round Cape Agulhas, a most insignificant-looking point covered with scrub and boulders, they were in fact passing the southern extremity of Africa at latitude 34° 50′ south. For all the maps based on the voyage of Dias showed the more spectacular Cape of Good Hope as being the tip of Africa. Even Álvaro Velho on the voyage of Vasco da Gama did not consider Cape Agulhas worthy of mention, and as late as 1505 Pacheco Pereira was still declaring that at the Cape of Good Hope the African continent came to an end.

Beyond Cape Agulhas Dias sailed past a coast bitten by many bays and coves, with sea-lion covered islands, and sand dunes intermingled with rocky promontories. Though little is indicated here on the maps, the mariners cannot have missed the spectacular headlands of this part of the coast and particularly the appropriately named Danger Point, which projects far out from the general coastline and rises to a height of over 200 feet, with the mass of Duinfonteinsberg rising behind it. There are off-lying perils, notably the submerged rock, a mile off the point, which the transport

Birkenhead struck in 1852, sinking with the loss of 445 lives. But Dias and his men escaped these dangers.

North-west of Danger Point, the caravels sailed into the wide expanse of Walker Bay, backed by great sandhills beyond which the modern seashore resort of Hermanus now sprawls along a line of low cliffs, and rounding Mudge Point, they came to the sandy bay at the head of which is the extensive lagoon that forms the mouth of the Bot River. They sailed on past a backdrop of mountains, the Paardeberg, the Blousteenberge and Kogelberg ranges, which exceed 4,000 feet, and beyond them the Hottentot Holland mountains which culminate in Sneeukop, with an altitude of 5,221 feet.

They were now nearing what they imagined to be the southernmost point of the continent as they sailed around Cape Hangklip, a low and sandy point jutting out from the sheer and often overhanging mass—1,400 feet high—of the Hangklipberg. To sixteenth-century Portuguese navigators Cape Hangklip became known as Cabo Falso—the False Cape—since pilots homeward bound would sometimes mistake it for the Cape of Good Hope and steer north, only to find their ship trapped in False Bay, which Dias appropriately named the Golfo dentro das Serras—the Bay between the Ranges.

The Cape of Good Hope forms the western rampart that shelters False Bay from the winds of the Atlantic. There is a familiar legend (which originates with the chronicler Barros who was doubtless anxious to please his courtly patrons) that Dias gave the 'great and notable Cape' the name of Cabo Tormentoso, or the Cape of Storms, because of the gales and dangers he had encountered in doubling it, and it was King João II who gave it the more illustrious name of Cabo da Boã Esperança, because it gave promise of the discovery of the sea route to India, which for so many years had been that monarch's elusive goal.

It is a good story, but it cannot be sustained. Pacheco Pereira, as we have seen, sailed home with Dias from west Africa in 1488, and he was therefore closer to the event than any other writer whose account has survived. His statement on this particular matter is quite unequivocal. 'It was not without good reason,' he tells us, 'that this promontory received the name Cabo da Boã Esperança because Bartolomeu Dias, who discovered it at the command of the late king João in the year 1488, saw that the coast here turned northwards and north-eastwards towards Ethiopia-under-Egypt and on to the gulf of Arabia, which gave indication and expectation of the discovery of India, and for this reason gave it the name of the Cabo da Boã Esperança.' A marginal note already referred to in one of the books that belonged to Christopher Columbus bears out the information given by Pacheco Pereira, for it records that Dias gave an account to King João of how he had navigated 'to the promontory called by him the Cabo da Boã Esperança'.

The Cape of Good Hope terminates in twin points. The western one, cliff-faced Cape Maclear, is 266 feet high; from here the coast runs north. Cape Maclear is separated by a shallow bight from the much bolder Cape Point, a mile and a quarter away, which falls sheer into the sea from a height of 687 feet; a mile and a half up the peninsula is a hill rising to 800 feet. The prominence of the Cape of Good Hope, and the fact that Dias believed it to be the southernmost point of Africa, would have made it an obvious place for the erection of a *padrão*, and Barros states that such a monument was indeed placed there. He records that Dias, after noting everything that was convenient to navigation, erected a *padrão* which he dedicated to São Filipe, and afterwards, because the *tempo*, which can mean either 'time' or 'weather', gave him no opportunity of landing, continued up the coast to rejoin his storeship. On the reverse of the same folio Barros listed the *padrões* erected by Cão and Dias, and repeated that Dias erected the *padrão* of São Filipe on the Cape of Good Hope.

Furthermore, after the return of Vasco da Gama from his first voyage to India, King Manuel ordered the weaving of a tapestry that would record the major events in the discovery of the sea route to the east. The third picture was to show the Cape of Good Hope—the name which, Manuel declared—had replaced the Promontorium Prassum of Ptolemy. Included in the picture were to be herds of elephants, negroes, cattle, shepherds with their flocks and some houses built in the local style. Vasco da Gama's ships were to be shown rounding the Cape, on which was to be delineated a *padrão* with the royal coat of arms and a cross on top, the year in which the *padrão* was erected, and some legible lettering.

That Dias erected a monument on St. Philip's Day, the 6th June 1488, to mark his discovery of the Cape of Good Hope seems evident, but up to now the most intensive searches have failed to find a trace of it or to establish exactly where it was placed.

After my discovery of the *padrão* at Kwaaihoek, I hoped to be able to establish the positions of the other *padrões*, and in January 1939 Professor Fouché, whose interest in my inquiries remained high, drove me from Simonstown, the terminus of the railway from Cape Town, to a farm some five miles from Cape Point, which became my base for two weeks while I systematically searched the area for any sign of the missing *padrão*.

Cape Point proved to be a spectacular mass, with the waves boiling and churning constantly against the rocks that lay beneath its sheer cliffs. There was no spot at which Dias could have landed a boat and hauled ashore half a ton of Portuguese limestone. Between Cape Point and Cape Maclear, however, I saw a beach, Klein Buffels Bay, where a boat could have landed under calm conditions, and immediately north of Cape Maclear there was an even better landing, sheltered by the massive cliffs and by a patch of kelp from all winds but those from the north-west.

But on Cape Point I could find no sign whatever of a *padrão* or of a mound that might in any way indicate its site. I systematically searched all the prominent spots within six or seven miles of the Cape, but all to no avail, and eventually I returned to Cape Maclear, which originally had seemed the most promising site. There I eventually noticed, about sixty feet in distance from the highest point of the cape and ten feet below it in level, a low pile of rocks, half-covered by small bushes and set a few feet back from the edge of the cliff. In the middle of this pile there was a socket, filled with sand. When I had cleared it, I found at the bottom some rotted timber about a foot in length.

I began to wonder whether the cross had perhaps been a wooden one. On the explorations that had taken place before Cão's first voyage it had been customary to raise timber crosses, and Dias, after all, had raised such a perishable monument on St. Croix Island. Moreover, Vasco da Gama in 1497, when he reached Mossel Bay, raised both a stone *padrão* and a lofty timber cross constructed from the mizzen-mast of his storeship which was stripped in that bay. There was, after all, more than a hint in the account by Barros of bad weather at the time when the *padrão* was raised, and it seemed possible that a gale had prevented the unloading of the stone *padrão*, or that an attempt had been made to land the *padrão* and it has been lost in the surf. In that event, since Dias clearly considered the discovery of the Cape of Good Hope the most important incident on his voyage, it would have been logical for him to insist on commemorating it in the best way he could, which would be to float a spar ashore, improvise a cross from it and build a cairn of rocks around it to hold it upright.

But whether it was possible for wood to survive in such a place for almost 450 years seemed problematical, and I submitted samples of the rotting fragment I had found at the bottom of the cairn to the Forest Products Institute of the South African Division of Forestry. The report revealed that the wood was probably larch, which in fairly dry conditions and protected from insects, is extremely durable. Though there was some sign of fungus on the fragments I had submitted, there was no sign of attack by insects, and the botanist who prepared the report came to the conclusion that 'it would not be impossible for timber under the conditions in which the sample was found to have withstood complete disintegration for as long as 450 years.' Beyond that, in those days before the development of carbon-14 dating, it was virtually impossible to proceed. The most that I now knew was that Dias could have erected the wooden monument of which I had discovered a fragment.

But there were two circumstances that lessened the probability. Firstly, the pile of rocks was not on the highest point of Cape Maclear, which would have been the obvious site for a landmark. Secondly, on the chart prepared during the survey which Captain W. F. Owen directed in 1825 of the Cape region, I found a circle drawn on the exact location of the cairn I had discovered. It may have represented a cairn which the surveyors found already there, or it may have represented a beacon which they themselves erected. And it seemed more likely that, in sea air, wood would last 110 years than 450 years.

There was a further consideration that seemed finally to eliminate the possibility that this was the cross Dias erected. On 6th June, the Day of St. Philip on which the *padrão* is said to have been raised, the bad weather at which Barros hinted would mean a gale blowing from the north-west, and this would make it impossible not merely to land a stone monument but even to land a boat at all on the beach north of Cape Maclear. Even if Barros was wrong in suggesting that Dias did not invent the name of Cape of Good Hope, he may still be right in recording that the explorer referred to the Cape as 'tormentosa' or stormy, and the surprisingly widely spaced dates of the naming of features on this return journey suggest that Dias made a slow passage round the coast from Struys Bay, and may well have sought temporary shelter in False Bay. In this case he could have found a good anchorage in Buffels Bay, within False Bay itself and three miles north of Cape Point, where a sandy beach interrupts the line of rocks which extends almost continuously for a dozen miles north of the Cape. Indeed, if the weather were bad and the winds adverse, it would obviously be more practical to land the *padrão* in some such sheltered bay before rounding the Cape than to attempt it afterwards in the face of the full Atlantic winds. But, as I have said, Cape Point yielded up no relic and no clue.

My failure to find any conclusive evidence in 1939 left me unsatisfied, and seventeen years later in 1956 I returned with my wife to make an even more extensive search. For the name 'Cape of Good Hope' has always been applied to a considerable region around the Cape itself, and in view of this wide connotation we decided to visit and to examine exhaustively all the prominent features of the coastline from Cape Infanta westward to Cape Maclear. We arrived one December evening on the banks of the Breë River, and the next morning, after a sleepless night in a storm-sodden tent (we had been assured that 'it never rains in summer at the Cape') I walked along the cliffs and shore following the route trudged by João do Infante and Perestrêlo. Barring off Cape Infanta I found a barbed-wire fence and a notice: 'WARNING: Trespassers will be prosecuted: this means you.' I climbed through the fence and started probing the sand on the slopes of the point. A young man emerged from the sea. 'Can't you read?' he asked. After a little conversation, it emerged that his family was attempting to preserve against poachers a herd of exotic red deer which had been brought to this rather remote spot. When I explained my mission, the family were sympathetic and entertained me at their summer shack. I searched and probed all over the point, but there was no sign of a *padrão* or of any platform on which one might have been placed.

We moved westward, working systematically over every piece of ground on which a monument meant to be seen from off shore might have been placed. The points that flanked Struys Bay produced nothing, and Cape Agulhas, of which we had some hopes as the true southernmost point of Africa, proved equally barren. We then travelled around the coast towards Quoin Point, which both the chart and the *Africa Pilot* suggested might appeal to sailors as a prominent point. A map prepared by the Trigonometrical Survey showed a farm called Ratelrivier as being the nearest point of human habitation—five or six miles away—and we drove in that direction, stopping at a house by the roadside to ask for directions. When he heard that we wished to go to Ratelrivier, the occupant of the house remarked that first of all he would have to ask the Lord. He went in and turned the handle of a rustic telephone. A long conversation ensued, but eventually he returned. 'The Lord says it is all right,' he reported. 'You can go to Ratelrivier. And what is more, there is a seaside cottage on the farm, and he says you are welcome to use it.' We congratulated him on having a direct line to Divinity, only to discover that the owner of the farm was Lord de Saumarez, a descendant of Nelson's second-in-command at the Battle of the Nile.

We established ourselves in the cottage so hospitably offered, and the next morning I walked the four miles along the beach to Quoin Point. I saw no cairns or any other likely clues along the way, and on the point itself, at the very spot on which a Portuguese explorer might have erected a *padrão*, I found an unattended lighthouse that had apparently been placed there only a few months before. I scraped around with a spade under the lattice framework at its base, but found nothing. The next morning, when I returned to make a more thorough examination, I saw to my consternation the masts and funnel of a wreck projecting from the surf half a mile off the point. I began to fear that the light had not burnt the previous night, and that I might be accused of having sabotaged it. There were some fishermen on the nearby rocks, and I went down to talk to them. To my relief, they told me that the ship had struck an hour after dawn; there had been a little fog, but not enough to cloak the coast, and they presumed the owners were anxious to collect insurance. A passing ship had rescued the two boatloads of the crew and there had been no casualties. No, they replied to my further inquiries, they knew nothing of any structure on the point before the lighthouse was put there, and, indeed, my further digging revealed no trace whatever of a *padrão* ever having been raised there.

We went on to examine Danger Point, and Cape Hangklip, both of them prominent enough to attract a mariner's attention, but without the least result, and a final examination of Cape Point and Cape Maclear was equally fruitless. Since then we have returned to the area of the Cape of Good Hope, and made further and more extended searches. But all to no avail; the *padrão* which Dias raised to celebrate what he believed to be the southernmost point of Africa, the legendary Promontorium Prassum of Ptolemy of which the medieval navigators had so long dreamed, remains the only one of the seven monuments raised by these two early Portuguese explorers of which no trace has been discovered in modern times.

From the Cape of Good Hope Dias sailed northward, and if the winds allowed him to keep in shore he saw a beach backed by low hills, and beyond the hills a sandy flat country broken by lagoons and the mountains that form the walls of Hout Bay, which may well be the Porto Fragoso—the Rocky Port—that appears on one of the early maps; it is protected from all the sea winds except those from the south-west, but it is made hazardous to sailing ships by the local currents of air created by the surrounding mountains.

It is likely that Dias had to keep so far out to sea that he did not enter Table Bay, where Cape Town now stands, and which, when the north-west wind is blowing, presents a lee shore as many sailing ships were to find to their cost in subsequent centuries; in 1865, for instance, a gale threw no less than seventeen ships upon the beach here. That Dias avoided such perils is shown by the fact that in 1503, when António de Saldanha anchored in Table Bay, his pilots confessed that they were ignorant of their exact position, which suggests that the rutters with which they had been equipped, based on information gathered during the voyages of Dias and Vasco da Gama, contained no description of the Bay in spite of its remarkable table-topped mountain landmark. Because of the confusion about their exact position, Saldanha climbed Table Mountain and from its summit he saw the Cape of Good Hope. His men collected fresh water from a stream which fell into the Bay, known throughout the sixteenth century as the Aguada de Saldanha. In 1601 a Dutch captain transferred the name of Saldanha to a bay seventy miles to the north which there is no record of the Portuguese captain ever having entered, and the original Saldanha Bay became known from then on, to Dutch and English alike, as Table Bay. It was on the shore of this bay, in 1510, that the great Francisco de Almeida, returning from his viceroyalty in Portuguese India, met his miserable and unnecessary death in battle with the Hottentots.

Undoubtedly it was from Saldanha, not from Dias, that Pacheco Pereira gained the description he gave of the country around Table Bay as it appeared to the early Portuguese visitors. He recorded that many of the plants were identical with those of Portugal, and he listed mint, camomile and cress; there were also wild olives, oaks and heathers which resembled those of his native hills. The reason for the similarity, he explained, was that the Cape was in the same latitude as that of Lisbon—and the latitude he gave, 34° 30′ south, was correct to within eight miles. The seasons were reversed, he made haste to add, and the months from April to September were cold and stormy. While he disagreed with the commonly-held notion that this was the Promontorium Prassum of the Hellenistic geographers, he believed nevertheless that the mountains in the interior must be Ptolemy's Mountains of the Moon in which the Nile had its source. He described the native inhabitants of the region as heathen, bestial people, though not as black as the negroes of the Guinea coast; they wore skins and sandals of raw hide, and possessed many cows, sheep and goats.

North of Table Bay the low sandy coastline is carpeted in springtime with wild flowers and presents a blaze of colour, but even if he had sailed close in shore Dias would have seen merely the colourless and unremarkable coast of mid winter. The likelihood is, however, that he continued to keep a fair offing as he hastened northward, for he certainly did not see the entrance to the misnamed Saldanha Bay or the rocky, reefy coast that extends to St. Helena Bay. That he did not enter St. Helena Bay itself is shown by the fact that it was Vasco da Gama who first named it, in November 1497. Álvaro Velho records that Vasco da Gama and his men 'did not know how far we were from the Cape of Good Hope, except that Pero de Alenquer [who had been pilot to Dias] said that the most we could be was thirty leagues short of the Cape. The reason why he would not be certain about it was that he had left the Cape [with Dias] one morning and had passed by there at night with the wind astern, and that on the outward voyage they had passed by out to sea, and for those reasons he was not able to recognize where they were.' Gama's men landed a large astrolabe which they set up on a tripod; they shot the sun and calculated that they were thirty leagues short of the Cape of Good Hope. This was the exact distance, and the accuracy does credit not only to their calculations but to those of Dias and his pilots.

Off the coast of South-West Africa, Dias sailed closer to the shore, and on St. Christopher's Day, the 24th July, he re-entered Lüderitz Bay, where, on a point to the westward, he raised his last *padrão*—or, if like Barros one counts by distance from Portugal, his first.

*   *   *

The *padrão* at Lüderitz stood until the end of the eighteenth century, but by the early 1820s it had been overthrown and had already been damaged by souvenir hunters. In 1855 Captain Carew, commander of a ship which was collecting guano for the Cape Town firm of de Pass and Sinclair, carried away the four remaining visible fragments of the monument. One was obtained by Sir George Grey, the Governor of Cape Colony, who took it with him as a souvenir of South Africa when he became governor of New Zealand. Visconde Duprat, the Portuguese representative on the Mixed Commission for the Suppression of Slavery which sat in Cape Town in 1865, laid claim to the remaining fragments for Portugal, and the next year two pieces, which fitted together, were handed over to him and shipped to Portugal. They were first placed in the museum of the Naval School, but in 1892 they were presented to the Colonial and Ethnographical Museum of the Sociedade de Geografia de Lisboa. The fourth fragment remained in South Africa, and it is today preserved in the South African Museum in Cape Town.

The guano collectors left no description of where they found fragments, but soon after Lüderitz's agents arrived on the coast of South-West Africa in 1883 they determined to commemorate the first white man to land on those shores, and raised a spar on what they thought the most likely spot, a knoll of rock which comprises the north-westernmost part of what had come to be called Dias Point. Later the German authorities replaced the spar with a wooden cross, and in 1929, after the Union of South Africa had assumed the mandatory administration of the territory, this wooden cross was replaced by one of granite. But already, in 1918, Professor E. Moritz had argued that the original *padrão* 'was not erected on the isolated rocky hill which is almost surrounded by water and which lies on the north-western corner of Dias Point; . . . the original cross stood actually on the flat ridge on which the [Lüderitz] lighthouse now stands.' He had reached this conclusion after studying the British Admiralty Chart 632, which was based on a survey made by Captain Brady in 1821; on the chart appeared a view of the coast on which the cross was delineated. Many years later the Historical Monuments Commission for South-West Africa decided that Professor Moritz's arguments should be investigated, and in 1950 the Secretary of the Commission approached me with the suggestion that I might attempt to locate the exact site. I was away from South Africa at the time, but when I returned in 1952 I inquired whether the Commission's invitation still held good, and when a reply came in the affirmative I planned to visit Lüderitz in the winter of 1953.

In the meantime I set about tracing whatever documents might have a bearing on the fate of the *padrão* after Dias had erected it. There was, not surprisingly, no information at all in the Portuguese records, for this part of South-West Africa lay away from the sea route that was eventually used by ships sailing from Europe to India, and it was generally thought until the nineteenth century that there was nothing of value in the territory, which lacked even fresh water and firewood. João de Lisboa, early in the sixteenth century, was content merely to give the distance and bearing of the Angra das Voltas (Lüderitz Bay) from a certain cape to the north, and with noting that the bay could be recognized by the two islands which lay within it, and subsequent rutters ignored the bay entirely.

The next explicit published reference to Lüderitz Bay (which by now had received the absurdly inappropriate name of Angra Pequena—Little Bay) was in James Rennell's account, published in 1800, of the visit made by Captain Thompson and Sir Home Popham in 1786, when they 'saw a marble cross, on a rock near Angra Pequena, in latitude 26° 37' South. The cross had on it the arms of Portugal, but the inscription was not legible ... The marble had been taken from the adjacent rocks.' The final statement seemed to me improbable, since no case was known in which a *padrão* had been cut on the spot by Portuguese explorers, and my inquiries from the Geological Survey of South Africa in fact revealed that Dias Point at Lüderitz Bay was composed of Archaean gneiss, and that the nearest accessible limestone was some forty miles to the south. The 'marble' from which the cross was made could not therefore have been taken from 'the adjacent rocks'; it must have been brought there by Dias.

After the visit by Thompson and Popham there was no mention of the cross until the visit of H.M.S. *Barracouta*, under the command of Captain Vidal, in 1825. It is true that the sloop *Star* had visited the bay in 1795, but the survey then made did not mark the cross, and I discovered that the view of the *padrão* shown on the map prepared by Brady after the visit of the *Menai* in 1821 was in fact based on a drawing made by Captain Thompson in 1786. The Curator of the Hydrographic Department of the Admiralty, who gave me this information, also told me that what little information there was of the survey made in 1824 by J. F. Chapman, commander of the *Espiègle*, contained no reference to the cross.

Lieutenant Boteler of the *Barracouta*, on the other hand, gave a vivid description of how the ship was scudding at a great rate before a south-easterly gale off the south-west coast of Africa on the 21st November 1825. In the afternoon they saw the cross erected by Dias at the south entrance to

Angra Pequena; the ship sailed past it and anchored in the bay. Captain Vidal and Lieutenant Boteler went ashore to examine the cross and determine the longitude and latitude of the point.

'The sand brought off by the guests of wind was painful enough to the eyes on board,' Boteler remembered, 'but on shore it was far worse; for it swept along the surface of the rock in clouds, almost blinding us as we advanced against it to the summit of the small granite eminence on which Diaz erected his cross . . .

'This cross is said to have been standing forty years ago but we found it thrown down, evidently by design, as that part of the shaft in a rough state which had originally been buried in the rock remained unbroken; which never could have been the case, had it been turned over any other wise than by having previously been lifted up from its foundation. The motive of this shameful mutilation probably was to search for such coin as might be supposed to have been placed under the cross when first erected. Whether the spoiler afterwards strove to make some amends by setting up a portion of it again, I cannot pretend to determine; but such was the state in which we found it. A piece of the shaft, including the part originally placed in the ground, and altogether five feet and a half in length, was propped up by means of large stones placed against it, and crossed at the top by a broken fragment, which had originally formed the whole length of the shaft below the cross, six feet above the ground, and twenty-one inches under. Its shape was rounded on one side, but left square on the other, evidently for the purpose of inserting the inscription, which the unsparing hand of Time, during the lapse of nearly three centuries and a half, had so obliterated that scarcely the remnant of a letter was visible. The whole was of a coarse white marble, and in diameter eight inches one way, and eight and a half the other. In descending the eminence by a different and more craggy path than that which I had followed in going up, I suddenly came upon the cross; it was sixteen inches square on the flat side, and a projecting piece at the top, of the same form and thickness as the shaft below, had given the whole, when perfect, the desired appearance. On the flat of the cross was an inscription, but like that of the shaft, it was almost obliterated. By observation the latitude was ascertained to be 26° 38′ 18″ south, and the longitude 15° 00′ 32″ east.'

In 1828, when Captain Morrell visited the bay, part at least of the shaft appears still to have been propped up, for in the narrative of his voyage he refers to 'a high bluff point rendered conspicuous by a marble cross erected on the summit in 1486 by Bartholomew Diaz, a Portuguese navigator. The monument of his successful enterprise along the coast of Africa is still standing, after having braved the storms and heats of three centuries and a half.' But by the 1840s the shaft had fallen, for Captain T. E. Eden, in the account of his voyage to the region (curiously entitled *The Search for Nitre and the True Nature of the Guano*) refers to 'Pedestal Point which is a little to the south of Angra Pequena and so named from a pedestal formerly erected by Admiral Diaz but now no longer standing'. In 1845 Saisset, commander of *La Loire*, saw the remains and tried to raise the column, but the fragments were too broken. One fragment bore the remains of an inscription, but this was very worn. While descending from the site he saw another fragment, in the shape of a cube, which also bore vestiges of writing, but this too was illegible.

A somewhat more dubious reference to the *padrão* during the mid-nineteenth century appeared in 1851 in an issue of the *Saint Helena Advocate*. It told how a certain Captain Parker of the brig *Kirkwood* had visited the site and, removing a broken pillar and a pile of small blocks of marble, dug through an accumulation of guano. Then, according to the story, he found 'a deal box, upon opening which a man with his arms across his heart and looking us in the face was presented to our view. The features betrayed an expression of terror. His garments were light and his hands had not been used to hard work. We brought him and a portion of the cross to St. Helena.' This seemed an unlikely story but, to leave no clue untested, I wrote to St. Helena. The Government Secretary replied. 'Enquiries have been made and old records have been searched . . . but it is regretted that no reference to the cross can be traced.'

I was however led in a more profitable direction by the publication, at about the same time as I heard from St. Helena, of Professor Vincent Harlow's masterly work, *The Founding of the Second British Empire, 1763–1783*. There was a reference here which suggested the possibility of finding an earlier description of the still-standing cross than that written by Thompson or Popham. At the end of 1780 a rupture took place between Britain and the Netherlands, and because of the Netherlands' support of France at this time, communications with India were threatened. Accordingly in 1781, a fleet and a force of troops were dispatched to occupy the Cape, but Admiral George Johnstone was surprised in a neutral port of the Cape Verde Islands, and as a result of this encounter he lost the race to Table Bay. Even St. Helena, used by English ships as a place of refreshment and rendezvous, was placed in jeopardy, and the government in Whitehall requested the East India Company to investigate possible ports of call on the west and south-west coasts of Africa. In 1783, Professor Harlow noted, the Company sent out the *Swallow* with instructions to examine 'all proper Places on this side of the Cape of Good Hope, not in the possession of or frequented by Europeans, at which the Company's Ships may be supplied with water and refreshments on their outward and homeward bound Passages'. She was to make a special search for fresh water at Angra Pequena and establish relations with the natives so that provisions might be obtained. But Professor Harlow said nothing about the expedition except that the voyage was curtailed and no useful discovery made.

An inquiry to the Public Record Office resulted in the reply that, though the log of the *Swallow* should have been preserved in the India Office records, it had been established that no log for the years 1783–4 was known to have survived. Professor Harlow, to whom I also wrote, replied: '. . . concerning the voyage of the *Swallow*, I dismissed it "in a sentence", as you say, for the very good reason that I knew nothing about it!' He had searched for the log and journal himself in the India Office library, but had found no trace of it.

'But', Professor Harlow continued, 'I have some interesting —even exciting—information for you.' This was about the *Nautilus*, the ship on which Thompson and Popham sailed into Angra Pequena in 1786. 'The Journal *is* in the Public Record Office. It is entitled "Narrative of a Voyage performed in His Majesty's sloop Nautilus under my command for the purpose of investigating the Western Coast of South Africa". ' The log also existed and Professor Harlow had made copious extracts from it, which he proposed to use in the second volume of his book, published—alas—posthumously. He sent me a passage describing Angra Pequena.

Captain Thompson wrote thus. 'Upon the westernmost

point which formed the bay of Pequena (which I named Pedestal Point) stands a cross, wrought of the natural marble of the Country, the face of which is to the westward, and is pretty conspicuous to a ship running along shore. On the Eastern and Western sides is an inscription neatly carved in old Roman characters, but the marble of which the Cross is made being of a very brittle quality, by age the inscription is wholly defaced, but on the end of the arms which points to the South, I plainly made out the Arms of Portugal, tho' also somewhat injured by pieces of the stone having dropped off: the carving of this pedestal is far from being rude, and it must have cost some time in erecting; the foundation of the stone (which is secured by a cement of mud and sand) is so mouldered by age that, tho' marble, it may be crumbled to dust by the finger.'

If Captain Thompson's assumptions were indeed correct, this was very significant information. Not only was the general shape of the *padrão* markedly different from that of those erected by Cão, and even from that erected by Dias at Kwaaihoek and reconstructed on the basis of surviving fragments, but there had been a dramatic departure from established practice in the carving of the arms of Portugal at the end of a cross-piece. Was it possible, one could not help speculating, for two crosses carried on the same voyage to be so different as the Lüderitz *padrão* as described and drawn by Captain Thompson and the Kwaaihoek *padrão* as reconstructed by the archaeologists in Johannesburg?

The log of the *Nautilus* provided another clue, for it went on to describe 'a fine spar', nineteen or twenty feet high, which had been erected on the west side of Angra Pequena to commemorate a visit by the French frigate *Venus*, commanded by Lieutenant Bart, in 1733. I immediately began to wonder whether Bart had described the *padrão* even before

Thompson and Popham, and whether he had made any notation of its exact position. The Bibliothèque Nationale of France could locate neither the log nor the journal of the *Venus*.

Before actually visiting Lüderitz I tried the only remaining avenue of inquiry that seemed at all promising. Sir George Grey had acquired a fragment of the *padrão* in the 1850s and had taken it with him to New Zealand; his collection had passed into the possession of the Auckland Library and Art Gallery. It struck me, first of all, that Sir George might have recorded some facts about the *padrão* that had since been lost; I was also anxious to obtain whatever information might exist about the shape, size and general appearance of the fragment he had acquired. But neither Sir George's notes—if he made any—nor the piece itself came to light; it appears to have been lost irremediably.

In June 1953, my wife and I set out for Lüderitz, driving from Cape Province, and on our first night in South-West Africa we stopped at a town on the edge of the diamond-prospecting zone. While we unpacked our car, a bearded man stood watching us inquisitively, and as we unloaded shovels, sieves and probing rod, he began to interrogate us about them. He turned out to be a security officer of the diamond-mining company which owned the rights over this area, and he demanded to know where we were going, and what was our purpose. The situation was not improved when our three-year-old daughter told him that I intended to dig up special stones. It was only after I had proved my connection with Dr. Cecil Lemmer, Chairman of the Commission for the Preservation of Natural and Historical Monuments of South-West Africa, that he accepted our *bona fides*. The next day, crossing the Namib desert, we passed at regular intervals the notices that were almost the only distinguishing features in that fascinating waste land. Each of them read, in English, Afrikaans and German:

WARNING!
PENALTY OF £500 OR ONE YEAR'S IMPRISONMENT
PROHIBITED DIAMOND AREA
KEEP TO THE ROAD

Lüderitz was a treeless town of steep-roofed grey stone buildings set on sandy slopes and a stony hillside. There we met Dr. Lemmer, and immediately he guided us the ten miles to Dias Point. The road ran southward across salty sand flats to the tip of the bay, and then north-westward, overshadowed by black-topped hills. The tide was high, and the isthmus that led to the peninsula of Dias Point was under water, so we left the car and waded the last few hundred yards. Above, on our right, rose the lighthouse ridge, but it was evident that this did not meet Rennell's account of Thompson and Popham having seen the cross set on a rock, or Boteler's talk of a small eminence. These descriptions, however, did seem to fit the knoll that stood away from the rest of the headland, separated by a channel which was swept by the seas at high tide and in north-westerly gales. A wooden footbridge spanned the channel, from which steps ascended the rock to provide the lighthouse keeper with access to the fog-horn which was housed in a fantastic painted wooden miniature of a German castle on the crest of the knoll. A few yards below the crest, on the landward side, stood a small building of corrugated iron resembling an outdoor earth closet; it actually housed the cylinders of compressed air which operated the fog-horn.

Beside the fog-horn stood the cross erected in 1929. From here we looked down the steep smooth slope of the rock into the sea, and back over the channel to the lighthouse ridge.

It seemed an admirable site for a *padrão*; in fact the crest of this half-island reminded me strongly of Kwaaihoek. The knoll was composed of gneiss, mainly black in colour, with a few veins of quartz. It was only fifty-five feet high, but it obviously stood out prominently against the sandy brown lighthouse ridge in the view of observers out at sea. On top of it a bright limestone cross would have been most conspicuous. Here the *padrão* would certainly have been battered by the winds and spray, as Thompson and Boteler stated; the wonder was that it had stood upright until the end of the eighteenth century. In spite of the view of Professor Moritz, I felt no doubt that this, and not the lighthouse ridge, was where Dias had erected his monument.

We scrambled down, glancing at the ledges on the way, and started fossicking among the rocks exposed by the outgoing tide. Wedged under one of them I saw a piece of the familiar limestone, standing out from the local stone by its colour, shape and texture. It had two parallel faces, so true that they had obviously been sawed. The broken faces revealed fossilized oyster shells, reminiscent of those in the Kwaaihoek fragments. Measurement showed the fragment to be 9 inches across at its broadest, and $8\frac{3}{4}$ inches at its thinnest; it tapered slightly, and the dimensions matched those of the fragments of the Lüderitz *padrão* in the South African Museum and the Sociedade de Geographia in Lisbon. The length of the piece was $8\frac{1}{2}$ inches, and it weighed —we found subsequently—approximately 16 pounds.

Dr. Lemmer was sceptical when I assured him that this was part of the *padrão*, and when my wife assured him that half of old Lisbon was built of such rock he refused to accept this as a valid scientific argument. The next day, however, his doubts were dramatically dispersed, for he himself found, below high-water mark in a crack where the channel entered the sea, a block of the same rock whose upper face bore the remains of an inscription. The writing was too worn and fragmentary to be read, but the traces of some five letters could be made out clearly. The style was identical with that of the Kwaaihoek inscription. The new block was just over 8 inches wide and a little less than 16 inches long. The back was broken and uneven, and the greatest depth was 5¾ inches. It weighed a massive 47 pounds.

That day and the next the three of us found more fragments, all wedged in cracks or under rocks. In all, these pieces, found below high-water mark, weighed 110 pounds, while the three largest, excluding the inscribed block, were found to fit together; they made up a total length of a shade less than 31½ inches.

I was anxious to look at Dias Point from the sea and compare the views sketched by Captain Thompson of the *Nautilus* of 1786, and appearing later on Chart 632, with the actual present-day profiles. The crawfish research vessel belonging to the Administration of South-West Africa—and appropriately named the *Nautilus*—was placed at our disposal, and sailing off shore one afternoon we satisfied ourselves of the faithfulness of Thompson's delineation. He had—as so often happens in topographical sketches—exaggerated the height in proportion to the other dimensions, and a precarious-looking overhang had obviously collapsed, but there remained a convincing similarity between the eighteenth-century representation and present appearances, and this strengthened our conviction that the *padrão* had indeed been placed on the fog-horn knoll.

After our off-shore reconnaissance, Dr. Lemmer had to return to Windhoek, the capital of South-West Africa, but my wife and I remained for a fortnight at Lüderitz and systematically probed and searched every crack and ledge on the knoll, in the channel and in the adjacent shallows. Altogether, by carefully sieving the sand and stones from various cracks and deposits, we collected more than 180 chips and pieces. The most interesting piece, which we found at the foot of the hillock, weighed about 4½ pounds and had two faces meeting at a right-angle. On one face, beginning at about 3 inches from the edge, there were traces of a worked recess, which suggested a socket. This piece could have been from the top of the shaft, in which case the base of the cross would have fitted into it: there could have been no intervening block as in the Cão *padrões*.

In my report to the Monuments Commission I had no hesitation in stating that the evidence of the views shown on Chart 632, taken in connection with the discovery of so many fragments of limestone that could only belong to the *padrão*, confirmed that the monument almost certainly stood approximately where the fog-horn house had been built; I suggested that beneath the concrete base of the house there might lie further fragments and perhaps even vestiges of the original platform. I pointed out, since most of the shaft had now been accounted for, but the cross had not yet been recovered, that further fragments might still be concealed, either in the channel beside the knoll or out to sea. I further expressed the view that it was unlikely that there had ever been a block between shaft and cross as in the case of the Cão *padrões*.

Shortly afterwards *The Times* of London carried a brief notice of our search, including a reference to Captain Thompson, and this resulted in a letter from Quentin Keynes (a grandson of Charles Darwin) who told me that he had in his possession Thompson's original manuscript, which included eight water-colour sketches and one actually depicted the Dias cross. Later he sent me a transcription of the entry in Thompson's manuscript describing the visit to Angra Pequena (which differed only in small details from that in the Public Record Office) and a photograph of the sketch of the cross.

Thompson's sketch—'The cross on Pedestal Point'—was both interesting and highly puzzling. It showed a traditional wooden cross rendered into stone, without a block, and with an inscription running across the front of the cross, and the Portuguese coat of arms (as Thompson had described it in his account) at the end of the exposed arm. This form was completely different from any of Cão's *padrões* and also from the reconstruction of the Dias monument at Kwaaihoek. Was it possible that Thompson had drawn this sketch from memory, and that his memory had played him false?

The only other contemporary evidence that could be found was contained in the journal kept by Home Popham when he was serving as Thompson's lieutenant on the *Nautilus*, which had also come into the possession of Mr. Keynes. Popham mentioned that the Dias cross stood on 'a round rock' and added that Captain Thompson 'ordered me to bring it on board if practicable. This I was soon convinced could not be done in an instant.' He sailed a ship's boat into the bay on the east side of Dias Point, found good anchorage in from six to nine fathoms within a quarter of a mile of the shore, and 'after walking over the Neck of Land that formed the Western part of the Bay, I found it was a Pedestal of Marble fixed on the Eminence of a round Rock the most conspicuous as a Mark to Seaward; on one of the Squares was engraved the Arms of Portugal, and on another some old characters, but both defaced by the Injury of the Weather, and the length of Time it had probably been erected'. But, since Popham does not make clear exactly what he means by 'Squares' it is impossible to envisage the shape of the monument clearly from his description. Later in his journal, Popham records that Captain Thompson 'told me he had been to the Cross, and had made out the Arms to be those of Portugal; the Characters old roman and much defaced, and the Pedestal worked from the Marble of the Country', which was obviously the source of Rennell's statement.

The fragments of the *padrão* were delivered to the Monuments Commission in Windhoek, and later on Dr. Lemmer took the block with the recess to Pretoria, where it was subjected to spectroscopic tests. It was found that the face of the socket showed a strong lead reaction, while elsewhere the lead reaction was slight. From this it appeared almost certain that the cross proper, of slender proportions, had been fixed directly into the top of the pillar without any intervening block, and that the *padrão* at Lüderitz had in fact been of the same shape as that which I discovered at Kwaaihoek. But Thompson's sketch indicated no such delicate shape, which made me all the more sceptical of it and all the more anxious to discover a sketch or an exact description by some other early visitor to the site. So far neither has emerged, nor has any fragment come to light either of a small cross that might have been mounted on the head of the shaft or a heavy cross-beam like that shown by Thompson. Thus, though the site of the third cross which Dias raised was clearly established by the search at Lüderitz, its exact form, and the inscription it bore, alike remain in doubt.

Sailing northward from Lüderitz, Dias returned to the bay where he had left the storeship, and found that of the nine men aboard six had perished at the hands of natives who, according to Barros, 'had coveted their trade-goods'.

It is of course possible that the behaviour of the Portuguese may not have been beyond reproach, and equally possible that a failure of mutual understanding had resulted in a clash over limited resources of fresh water or fresh meat. Be that as it may, one of the three men who was still alive when Dias returned was so overcome with joy at the sight of his companions that he dropped down dead; he was the purser, Fernão Colaço. The remaining contents of the storeship were transferred to the caravels, and, since there were too few hands to work three vessels, she was set on fire.

It is possible, as we have already seen, that Dias put in at the mouth of the Congo on his return voyage, and that it was he who conveyed to Portugal the King of Congo's ambassador, Caçuto. He certainly called at Principe Island in the Gulf of Guinea and rescued Pacheco Pereira, who had been sent to explore the rivers which enter the Bight of Biafra and which only in the nineteenth century were proved to be the various mouths of the Niger. Falling ill of fever, Pacheco Pereira had sent his crew to trade on the mainland, but there they lost their vessel; the survivors had managed to rejoin Pereira on Principe, and they were greatly relieved to see the sails of Dias's ships and to be taken on board. Doubtless on the advice of Pacheco Pereira, Dias turned aside from his route home to trade for gold at the mouth of one of the rivers on the mainland, handing over the product of his commerce to the factor at São Jorge da Mina where, as was customary, he stopped for his men to refresh themselves on European food and drink and other comforts.

Dias returned to the Tagus, as we have seen, in December 1488, having been sixteen months and seventeen days on his voyage, and having discovered 350 leagues of unknown coastline, which was double that discovered by Diogo Cão. He was welcomed with enthusiasm, but, curiously, there is no record of his having received any special reward or honour at the hands of King João, to the achievement of whose ambitions for Portugal his discovery so notably contributed.

A note of his return, written in the margin of a printed book probably by Christopher Columbus, or possibly by his brother Bartholomew, to which I have already referred in passing, gives an interesting sidelight on the event.

'Note that in the month of December of this year 1488, there reached Lisbon Bartolomeu Dias, captain of three caravels, who had been sent by the most serene king of Portugal to Guinea to discover lands; and he recounted to the same most serene king that he navigated six hundred leagues beyond that already navigated, i.e. 450 leagues to the south and 250 leagues to the north, to the promontory called by him the Cabo da Boa Eperança, which we supposed to be situated in Agesinba [Abyssinia]: and this place he knew by astrolabe to be distant from the equinoctial line 450; this last place was distant 3,100 leagues from Lisbon; this voyage he sketched and wrote, league by league, in a chart for the most serene king to see with his own eyes; and in all these things I was present.'

The latitude which Columbus gives is of course ten degrees in error, and it may well be that Dias and the King deliberately misled him, to convince him and the monarch of Castile (with whom Christopher Columbus was then negotiating for patronage) that the route Dias had discovered went far south and provided no easy way to the East.

The chart which Dias made for the King has perished, though many of its notations found their way, doubtless through Spanish and Italian spies, onto other early maps. But even in the absence of such first-hand evidence, enough is known not only to show that it was he who proved the existence of a feasible sea route to the Indian Ocean, but also that he discovered the south-east trade winds and the westerlies to the west and south of South Africa, thus establishing the wind system that the Portuguese, and the Dutch and British after them, would use on their voyages to Asia until the advent of the steamship more than three centuries after the discovery of the Cape of Good Hope.

VII

The Aftermath and the Death of Dias

THE first consequence of the voyages and the discoveries of
Cão and Dias was not an immediate opening of the sea route
to India, but the establishment of Portuguese influence in
the kingdom of Congo. The embassy from the King of Congo
to the King of Portugal, which Dias—or just possibly the
leader of some other expedition whose records have been
completely lost—conveyed to the Tagus, was headed by the
man whom the Portuguese chroniclers call Caçuto; his real
name, according to modern scholars, was Nsaku, and he was
a man of some importance among his people. As one of the
hostages whom Cão had taken to Portugal, he had been
mainly responsible for establishing in his own King's mind a
sense of the marvels of European life and of the probable
advantages of an alliance with a people so powerful as the
Portuguese.

The embassy met King João II in the Portuguese town of
Beja at the beginning of 1489, and Nsaku offered presents
from his royal master, Nzinga a Nkuwu: tusks of ivory, finely
worked ivory artefacts and fine fabrics woven from raffia
fibres. He then repeated his King's wish that João should
send to the Congo priests, stonemasons and carpenters,
farmers adept in husbandry and tillage, and women to
teach the baking of bread. The King also asked that certain
youths he had sent with his embassy be taught the Portuguese

language and Portuguese customs so that on their return they might educate their fellows.

King João and his Queen stood as godparents when Nsaku and his company were baptized, and he kept them in Portugal until the end of 1490 so that they could become familiar with Christian ways and the Portuguese tongue. Then he appointed as his own ambassador to the Congo a nobleman with service at sea, Gonçalo de Sousa, and instructed a number of friars of various orders and secular priests, carpenters and stonemasons, to accompany him so that the King of Congo's requests might be fulfilled. The two delegations left Portugal in December 1490. Off Cape Verde, however, Gonçalo de Sousa died of plague he had contracted in Lisbon, and soon afterwards Nsaku and several of the Congolese youths succumbed to the same sickness. The remaining Portuguese were dismayed by this tragic turn of events, and they put into one of the harbours of the Cape Verde Islands where the captains, masters and pilots of the ships met in council. It was decided to continue their mission and Rui de Sousa, a nephew of the dead ambassador, was elected their new commander.

They reached the Congo on the 29th March 1491, and anchored in the lee of the Ponta do Padrão. It was familiar country to two of the pilots, Pero de Alenquer who had accompanied Dias, and Pero Escolar who had served under Cão. The local chief or *mani*, Soyo, whose kraal lay two leagues inland, received cordially the messengers who took him word of the return of the surviving Congolese and the arrival of the Portuguese delegation, and when the main party landed, with trumpets playing and armed with crossbows, lances and firearms, he staged a great celebration, in which 3,000 warriors armed with bows and arrows danced to the accompaniment of throbbing drums. They were naked from the waist up, painted in white and other colours, while below the waist they wore brightly coloured palm cloths. On their heads were parrot f:athers, while Soyo himself wore a remarkable cap which bore a cunningly-worked representation of a snake.

Soyo occupied a strategic but at the same time vulnerable position as chief of the province that controlled the lower reaches of the Congo, and he immediately decided to throw in his lot with these powerful foreigners. Within a few days, on the 3rd April, he manifested his good will by accepting baptism, and when the Portuguese departed for the *mbanza* Congo, the King's capital, he supplied 200 porters to serve their personal needs and others to carry the provisions he had provided, while from among his warriors an escort was recruited to prevent attack by bandits along the way.

The journey inland went at a leisurely pace, and it was twenty-three days before they reached the capital, where the King of Congo received them with great celebrations, and Rui de Sousa offered King João's present of brocades and silks, velvets and damasks. Nzinga a Nkuwu was delighted at the arrival of the friars, priests and craftsmen, and immediately he ordered 1,000 of his own men to assist them in the construction of a church. The work of assembling stones, some of which had to be brought two or three leagues, began on the 6th May 1491, but when Nzinga heard that Soyo had already been baptized, he decided that he could not wait to accept this new and obviously powerful fetish until the church had been completed. He was baptized in May, adopting the name of his brother-King João, and with him were christened six men of his family, each of them the chief of an outlying province who could put 10,000 warriors in the field of battle. Nzinga's principal wife soon followed his example, taking the name of Leonor, the Queen of Portugal, while his son who was chief of the upriver province of Nsundi, adopted the name of Afonso.

The King then hurried off to quell a rebellion up the river. Rui de Sousa formally presented him with a banner bearing the cross of Christ, since Nzinga was now among the Christian monarchs, and the King of Portugal was his ally. De Sousa gave the King physical as well as spiritual assistance, for he also detached at least one and possibly more of his ships to sail up the river and give support to Nzinga's army. It is likely that Pero de Escolar, who had ascended the Congo with Cão, piloted the detachment, and it is probable that Portuguese gunfire gained the day for their allies. As soon as the expeditionary force returned to the mouth of the Congo, Rui de Sousa weighed anchor and sailed for Portugal, leaving behind at the Congolese court four clerics and at least one African who had learnt to read and write and who would help in teaching the young men attendant on the King both the Portuguese language and the courtly skills of Europe. 'There also remained', adds Rui de Pina in his account, 'other persons of distinction ordered to go by land and discover other distant countries, with India and Prester John as their objectives.'

Rui de Pina was writing very close to the events that make history, for he based the chapters of his *Cronica de Dom João II* on a report which he himself wrote in 1492, immediately after the return of the expedition to Lisbon, and after he had personally interviewed Rui de Sousa and six other participants in the delegation. The original of this report has perished, but a contemporary Italian version survives, made by a commercial agent—conceivably Jeronimo Sernigi, the Italian who lived for some years in Lisbon and in 1499 wrote a letter describing Vasco da Gama's voyage. This Italian translation of the report contains a passage which does not appear in Rui de Pina's chronicle as it was eventually printed, and which was presumably interpolated by the translator.

'The Spanish cosmographers think that this river rises in the Mountains of the Moon, where the Nile has its source, and they declare that there is nothing obscure about this origin, for there is the evidence of ancient cosmographers who say that the Nile rises there, and that another river also rises there which flows to the ocean sea. Accordingly, since this project promises, with the help of God, so much for the future, the Spaniards are searching and investigating the truth of this thing and the source of this river.'

Since there were no Spaniards on the Congo, it is clear that the translator is using the term generally to include all Iberians, and that his remark provides supporting evidence that the Portuguese left behind them in 1492 an exploring party with instructions to ascend the Congo, proceed to the sources of the Nile and establish contact with Prester John. No record of the fate of this expedition has survived.

King João was nothing if not persistent in his efforts to form an alliance with his fellow Christian monarch, and even while his explorers were probing up the valley of the Congo towards the semi-mythical kingdom of Ethiopia, he was awaiting news of another traveller, Pero da Covilhã, whom he had sent on a journey through the Levant towards Arabia and Abyssinia which complemented that on which Dias had been dispatched.

Pero was of obscure origin, for he bore only the name of the small mountain town in which he had been born. As a youth he served with the Duke of Medina Sidonia, acquiring in the process a knowledge not only of the military arts but also of the Andalusian dialect of Spanish. Later he entered the service of the Portuguese King Afonso, first as a groom and later as a squire; he proved his valour during that King's invasion of Castile. After Afonso's death he served João II.

Soon after João's accession his reign was threatened by a conspiracy of noblemen. Their leader was the Duke of Bragança, who entered into treasonable communication with the rulers of Spain; he was arrested in 1483 and executed in the following year, while his brother, the Marquês de Montemar, and other conspirators fled to Castile. After this, the Duke of Viseu, the Queen's brother and João's cousin, became the leader of the remaining conspirators, but their plan to assassinate João became known to him and he killed Viseu with his own hands; the Duke's accomplices were arrested and lodged in prison where a number of them soon died 'according to report not naturally, but artificially'. Others fled to Spain, and João now chose Pero da Covilhã to go as his secret agent and glean information about the intentions of the refugees. Pero, who appears to have been a natural linguist, had picked up Arabic from the *moriscos* during his service with the Duke of Medina Sidonia in Andulusia, and, after he had served his King well in spying on the exile conspirators, he was appointed to carry out a second confidential mission, this time in North Africa, where João sent him to Tlemcen, ostensibly to buy striped cloth which was much in demand as an item of trade on the Guinea coast, but also to hold secret talks with the ruler of that city to prevent him from aiding his neighbours to the west who were pressing on the Portuguese possessions in Morocco; Pero may also have been instructed to observe the diplomatic activities of the Spanish rulers in that region. Later he was sent on a further African mission, this time to Fez, ostensibly to buy horses, but once again with secret instructions whose exact nature is no longer known. On these two journeys he perfected his Arabic and, being a highly observant man, learnt much about Muslim customs.

On his return from this second African expedition, King João summoned Pero da Covilhã to his court in May 1487. What happened then was told by Father Francisco Álvares who met Pero in Ethiopia when the Portuguese mission visited that country in 1520. Father Francisco's account was included by the Italian geographer, Giovanni Battista Ramusio, in his famous collection of travel documents, *Navigationi e Viaggi* (the Italian equivalent of Hakluyt's *Voyages*), but Ramusio supplemented the cleric's statement with fragments of information derived from a report on Pero da Covilhã's travels which was given him by the Portuguese chronicler and humanist Damião de Gois. These interpolated fragments are shown by square brackets.

'When he arrived, the king spoke to him in great secrecy, telling him that he expected a great service of him, because he had always found him a good and faithful servant and fortunate in his acts and services [and because he knew Arabic well]; and this service was that he and another companion, who was named Afonso de Payva, should both go to discover and learn about the Prester John [and whether he bordered on the sea], and where [pepper and] cinnamon is to be found, and the other spices which from these parts went to Venice through the countries of the Moors; and that already he had sent on this journey a man of the house of Monterio and a friar named Fray Antonio, a native of Lisbon, and that they had both reached Jerusalem and had turned back there saying that it was not possible to go to those countries without knowledge of Arabic, and therefore he requested Pero da Covilhã [as he knew Arabic well] to accept this journey [and to do it as a special service, promising so to reward him that he would be a great man in

his kingdom and all his people should ever live in content-
ment], and to do this service with the said Afonso de Payva.
To which Pero da Covilhã answered that he [kissed His
Majesty's hands for the favour he showed him, and] regretted
that his capacity was not as great as his desire to serve His
Highness, and that [as a faithful servant] he accepted the
journey with alacrity.'

Prince Manuel, who would soon succeed João II as King
of Portugal, was present at the meeting and gave Pero da
Covilhã and his companion Afonso de Paiva a chart that
had been drawn up by three noted cosmographers, Ortiz de
Vilhegas, Bishop of Vizeu, Dr. Rodrigo and Dr. Moses.
They had, as Ramusio tells us, 'shown as well as they could
how they would have to set about going and finding the
countries the spices came from, and how one of them could
go to Ethiopia to see the Prester John's country and see
whether in his seas there was any knowledge of a passage to
the western seas, for those doctors said they had found some
memorial or other about that'.

The King gave Pero da Covilhã and Afonso de Paiva 400
cruzados in cash and a letter of credit valid for any country
in the Levant. They travelled by way of Barcelona and
Naples to Rhodes, where they bought a quantity of honey
which enabled them to arrive in Alexandria posing as
merchants. There they both fell ill, and came so close to
death that the governor, in anticipation of that eventuality,
took possession of their goods. On their recovery they bought
more trade-goods and proceeded to Cairo, where they
awaited the arrival of merchants from Fez and Tlemcen,
and in their company caravanned to the head of the Red
Sea and down to Toro, where they took boat to Suakim and
Aden.

At Aden, which even then was an important shipping

centre, vital to the Arab trade with the Indies, they parted company. Paiva returned to Africa to carry on the quest for Prester John, while Pero da Covilhã transhipped to a larger dhow which sailed with the south-west monsoon across the Arabian Sea to the Malabar coast of India. He landed at Cannanore and thence travelled to Calicut, the capital of a Hindu state which had acquired importance because of its central position in Malabar. Pero da Covilhã discovered that pepper and ginger were grown in the locality, but that cloves and cinnamon were brought by Arab merchants from more distant countries, so that Calicut had become the great centre of the spice trade, to which came ships from the East Indies and even junks from China. Pero travelled northward to Goa, which possessed the best port on the coast of west India; it was the place of import for Arabian horses which were sold to the rajas of India. On the Malabar coast Pero also heard of the commercial importance of Hormuz, which was situated on an island in the throat of the Persian Gulf; all the spices destined for Europe which did not go via Aden and Alexandria were taken past Hormuz to the head of the Gulf, and thence by caravan to the eastern Mediterranean.

Pero found his way to Hormuz, and there he learnt about the trading routes between the nearby Arabian sultanate of Oman and the coast of East Africa. He heard also of the gold produced in great quantities in the lands of King Mono-motapa, which lay to the south of the Lower Zambesi, and of the city of Kilwa, with its magnificent buildings, which had become prosperous through this trade.

Adept in plausible disguises, Pero was able to board one of the ships that sailed to East Africa, where he was anxious to discover how far south the Arabs sailed and also to compare the actual coast with the chart which Prince Manuel had given him. The dhow on which he travelled probably called at Mogadishu and Brava on the Somali coast, at either Malindi or Mombasa in present-day Kenya, and at Zanzibar, before anchoring in the deep harbour at Kilwa where the Friday mosque with its many cupolas must have reminded him of that in Cordoba, which he had seen on his visits to Andalusia. On this or another ship he proceeded southward to the picturesque island of Moçambique, which gave shelter from the monsoon winds, and the town of Sofala beside its rapidly shoaling river. There, according to Ramusio, 'he learnt from sailors and from some Arabs that the whole coast to the west could be navigated and that its end was not known.'

Having gathered much vital information, Pero da Covilhã took ship northward as soon as the monsoon permitted, and by way of Zeila and Toro he reached Cairo, probably in 1490. There he sought news of Paiva, only to learn that his companion had died in an unsuccessful attempt to reach Abyssinia. He was about to return to Portugal when two messengers from that country found him and gave him letters from King João. The King intimated that if the mission had been completely successful, Pero da Covilhã and Afonso de Paiva should return home, where they would be warmly welcomed and duly rewarded. But if by any chance they had not wholly complied with their instructions, especially those regarding the discovery of the land of Prester John, they were to send a report of what they had done and to labour to complete the balance of their mission. Moreover, they were to conduct one of the messengers to Hormuz, so that he could carry out a special mission there.

The two messengers were Portuguese Jews. One of them, Joseph, had already been on a journey to Baghdad, where he had heard of the importance of Hormuz, and on his return to Portugal he had reported this to King João; it was the second messenger, Rabbi Abraham, who was charged with the mission of visiting Hormuz and assessing its strategic importance in terms of Asian commerce.

Pero da Covilhã sadly accepted these new instructions, but before setting off down the Red Sea he wrote a full report to his King on what he had seen and learnt since he left Portugal.

According to Father Francisco Álvares, who based his account on a conversation with Pero some thirty years after the events, he described 'how he had discovered cinnamon and pepper in the city of Calecut, and that cloves came from beyond, but that all could be had there; and that he had been in the said cities of Cananor [Cannanore?], Calecut and Goa, all on the coast, and to this they could well navigate by their coast and the seas of Guinea, making for the coast of Sofala, to which he had also gone, or a great island which the Moors call the Island of the Moon [Madagascar]; they say that it has 300 leagues of coast, and that from each of these lands one could fetch the coast of Calecut.'

Ramusio's version is slightly but significantly different; he records that Pero told the King 'about all that he had seen along the coast of Calicut, and about the spices, and Hormuz, and the coast of Ethiopia, and Cefala, and the big island, saying finally that his caravels, which were accustomed to sail to Guinea, if they navigated along the coast and asked for the coast of that island and of Cefala, could easily penetrate to those eastern seas and reach the coast of Calicut, for it was sea all the way, as he had learned'.

Having seen Joseph on his way back to Portugal, Pero da Covilhã conducted Abraham to Hormuz, whence the Rabbi doubtless proceeded to Basrah at the head of the Persian Gulf and accompanied a caravan to the eastern

Mediterranean. Pero returned to the Red Sea aboard a vessel which called at the port of Jiddah in the Hejaz, and there he took the opportunity to penetrate into the heart of the Islamic world, for he joined a party of pilgrims and so excellent was his disguise that he became the first European ever known to have visited Mecca. He went on to Sinai and Toro, and from Zeila he travelled inland to the court of the Emperor of Abyssinia. The reigning ruler, Alexander, received him hospitably, and promised to assist him to return to the coast. But Alexander was killed in a palace revolution, his seventeen-year-old successor died a few months later, and the later Neguses Nahum and David both appreciated Covilhã's qualities so much that they refused to let him depart. He was presented with estates and married a wealthy wife, and when the next Portuguese arrived in 1520 he was a person of authority.

Whether Joseph returned to Portugal with Pero's report, or whether Abraham survived the journey from Hormuz to the Mediterranean, is not now known. Certainly the fact that Vasco da Gama was sent out in 1497 bearing letters addressed specifically from King Manuel to the ruler of Calicut suggests that the information Pero collected did reach Lisbon, but it is possible that this information may have come through other channels, for, as several writers have pointed out, there were gaps in Vasco da Gama's knowledge of the regions to which he sailed that seem curious if one assumes the information Pero sent home was actually available to him. For example, he appears to have received no instructions to make further inquiries regarding the trade of Sofala, he expressed surprise at the high civilization of the Arab towns in the east coast of Africa, he confused Christian churches with Hindu temples on the Malabar coast, and he was provided with a trumpery selection of trade-goods which were quite unsuitable for the spice trade as it was conducted by the Arab merchants.

There is one other circumstance which at least suggests that King João waited long and in vain for news of Pero da Covilhã, and that is the long delay between the return of Dias in 1488 and the dispatch of Vasco da Gama by King Manuel in 1497. João, it seems probable, delayed Portuguese penetration into the Arabian Sea because he was waiting for news of the Christian King whom he might make his ally in that region separated from Europe by the Muslim world.

Nor can one ignore the concern which King João and his advisers felt over Spanish enterprises in the Atlantic, and particularly over the discoveries of Christopher Columbus, for whose achievements in the service of the rulers of Spain the Portuguese were at least partly responsible owing to their failure to assess the opportunity which Columbus once offered them.

Columbus's first link with Portugal was made in 1476, when he was on board a vessel in a Genoese convoy attacked near Cape St. Vincent by a combined French and Portuguese fleet. Columbus's ship was sunk, but he was able to reach the shore by supporting himself on a wooden sweep. He was treated hospitably by the people of Lagos in the Algarve, and after serving in a Portuguese ship that visited Iceland, he returned to Portugal and spent the next eight or nine years there. As Admiral Samuel E. Morison has pointed out in his definitive biography of the explorer, *Admiral of the Ocean Sea*, 'This lucky landing in Portugal was the turning point of Christopher's career, for chance had washed him ashore in the world-centre of oceanic voyages and discovery. He was among people who could teach him everything he was eager to learn: Portuguese and Castilian, the languages of far-ranging seamen; Latin to read the geographical works of the past; mathematics and astronomy for celestial navigation; shipbuilding and rigging; and above all discovery.'

It is possible that Columbus joined his brother Bartholomew in making charts in Lisbon. It is certain that he sailed to the islands of Madeira, where he met the daughter of the captain of Porto Santo and so married into the important and influential Perestrêlo family which, as we have seen, played a considerable part in the consolidation of Portuguese discoveries at the end of the sixteenth century. Somewhere between 1482 and 1484 he visited the Guinea coast, and it is possible that there or elsewhere he may have met Diogo Cão

Nevertheless, though he learnt many practical things and much good seamanship from the Portuguese, unlike them he was inclined to look to the west rather than to the east for a way to India. Fragments of carved wood, and pieces of types of bamboo not found in Africa had washed up, blown by the prevailing westerly winds, on the beaches of Madeira, and these clues strengthened in the mind of Columbus the idea of land existing to the west. He appears to have been influenced by seeing the copy of a letter which the Florentine physician and amateur cosmographer, Paolo Toscanelli, had written to King Afonso V (at Afonso's request) regarding the possibility of finding a western route to India. Overestimating the extent of Asia from Marco Polo's description, and under-estimating the circumference of the globe because he still held to Ptolemy's inaccurate calculations, Toscanelli had told Afonso that if a ship sailed 5,000 miles from Lisbon it would reach Cathay (or China), and that if it sailed by a different course 'to the island of Antillia which is known to you', it would be a mere 2,000 miles from there to Cipangu (or Japan). The advisers of Afonso and João II knew better, and so Cão was sent out on his second exploration to continue the search for an eastern route to India. But Columbus remained fascinated by the arguments of his fellow Italian, and even compounded the errors of Toscanelli by stretching Marco Polo's Asia still farther east; by reducing the value of a degree of longitude in actual nautical miles to about three-quarters of its true dimensions, he ended by convincing himself—though he convinced few others—that a mere sixty-eight degrees separated Cape St. Vincent in the Algarve from Japan.

In 1484 Columbus sought an audience with João II and requested that the King appoint him to the command of an expedition that would reach the East by sailing west. Recording this interview, the chronicler Barros describes Columbus as being 'skilful, eloquent, a good Latinist, and most vainglorious'. And he continues: 'The king gave him little credit, for he saw that this Cristovão Colom was a big talker and vainglorious in singing his own accomplishments, and fuller of fancy and imagination than of certainty, with his island of Cipangu. But such was the force of his importunities that the king ordered that he meet with Dom Ortiz [de Vilhegas], bishop of Ceuta, and with Master Rodrigo [the King's physician] and Master Josope [Vizinho, pupil of Abraham Zacuto] to whom he had committed these matters of cosmography and discovery; and they all held the words of Cristovão Colom to be vain and founded on imagination and things like the island of Cipangu of Marco Polo.'

Columbus transferred his importunities to the court of Queen Isabella of Castile. Nevertheless, in 1485, perhaps to make sure that he was missing no opportunity, King João authorized a Portuguese captain, Fernão Dulmo, to go in search of Antillia, the island of the Seven Cities beloved of medieval cosmographers, which Dulmo offered to do at his own expense, an arrangement much more acceptable to João than Columbus's grandiloquent and exorbitant demands. Unfortunately, nothing is known of the outcome of Dulmo's expedition.

In 1492, having won the patronage of Isabella, Columbus sailed west and discovered the Bahamas, Cuba and Hispaniola. On the return voyage severe storms assailed his two vessels, at times reaching hurricane intensity, but on the 4th March 1493 the Cabo da Roca, the westernmost point of Portugal and of Europe, came into view, and Columbus decided that he must put into the mouth of the Tagus to replace his torn sails. Accordingly, the *Niña* anchored off Restelo. A Portuguese warship, possibly the *São Cristovao*, was guarding this entrance to the harbour of Lisbon. The master of this ship was a Bartolomeu Dias, though it is not certain that he was the explorer. He demanded that Columbus accompany him to the guardship and show his papers to the captain. Columbus refused haughtily, arguing that it was to him, as Admiral of the Ocean Sea, that honours should be paid. Dias insisted on seeing the papers of the *Niña*; when he reported the incident to his captain, the latter paid a ceremonial call on Columbus, to the accompaniment of trumpets, drums and pipes. Meanwhile Dias was instrumental in transmitting a letter from Columbus to King João who, because of an outbreak of the plague in Lisbon, was lodging in a monastery at Val do Paraiso, near Santarem and some distance up the Tagus.

João ordered that the *Niña* and her crew be supplied with every necessity, and he invited Columbus to pay him a visit. There is no contemporary record of their conversation, but it is generally accepted, on the basis of the chronicles of Rui de Pina and Barros, that João reacted strongly to

Columbus's announcement. He declared that the territories discovered by Columbus lay within the area allocated to Portugal by the Treaty of Toledo in 1480, and he refused to discuss the matter further with Columbus, and declared that the question of sovereignty would be resolved by litigation between the Catholic monarchs of Portugal and Spain. He added that he would immediately dispatch an armada, under Francisco de Almeida (who had defeated a Spanish force at Granada during Afonso's war with Castile) to take possession of the lands discovered by Columbus.

In fact no such expedition was dispatched, and it seems likely that from this point began the negotiations which led to the Treaty of Tordesillas of 1494 in which, because of their superior knowledge of the value of a degree and the size of the earth, the Portuguese contrived to secure a remarkably good bargain for themselves. Since the boundary between the spheres of influence of the Catholic kings ran 370 leagues west of the Cape Verde Islands, this meant that Portugal would be able to claim the eastern bulge of South America, which became the rich colony of Brazil, while, though Spain gained the rest of the New World (which it was unable to keep intact against the probing initiatives of British, French and Netherlanders), it was effectively excluded from the rich trade of the Indies. It is very significant that only after the Treaty of Tordesillas did the Portuguese kings—João and Manuel—in fact prepare the expedition that would bring to fruition the discoveries of Diogo Cão and Bartolomeu Dias.

There is no doubt that such an expedition was contemplated as soon as Dias returned from the discovery of the Cape of Good Hope, and that it was delayed only by the uncertainty of Pero da Covilhã's success in establishing contact with Prester John and by the urgency of reaching an understanding with Spain that was imposed by Columbus's discovery of the New World.

When the expedition was organized the experience of Dias was freely called upon, and it was probably he who recommended that the caravels had served their purpose. The work of true exploration was now almost ended, and what would now be required were vessels of heavier burden which could carry a larger crew, more stores and a sufficient supply of trade-goods to try the spice market. Moreover, experience had shown that vessels bound for the Indies should be more robust and have a higher freeboard, the better to withstand gales off the South African coast. For this purpose square-rigged *naus*, which could also carry heavy artillery, would be more effective than the lateen-rigged caravels.

João II died in 1495; his final years had been clouded by deepening ill-health and by the accidental death of his only son Afonso while riding on the banks of the Tagus. He died at the age of forty and, though he would have preferred an illegitimate son to succeed him, it was his cousin and brother-in-law, Manuel, who actually ascended the throne and began one of the most brilliant reigns in Portuguese history, distinguished by its own style of architecture and by the spread of Portuguese power to the confines of the Chinese empire and the shores of Japan.

Long before he became king, Manuel had taken a keen interest in the progress of exploration, and João's mantle fitted well on his shoulders. But before he could implement the plans he had doubtless been forming during the years of waiting for the throne, he had to secure the support of the influential Portuguese families who could provide not only leadership but also capital for an adventurous policy of commercial and imperial expansion. Immediately after his accession, Manuel called a meeting of his council of state at which he presented the question of maritime discovery. According to Barros, most of them were sceptical. They criticized the length of the projected voyage around the Cape to India, its cost, its difficulties and—even if it were successful—the expense of maintaining Portuguese strength in the Indies at such a distance from home. If Portugal were successful in establishing trade with the Indies, they argued, it would only open the way for her rivals and competitors. Some of the councillors argued that the Portuguese royal house had been responsible for overseas exploration and expansion since 1415; it was a royal obligation, the duty of the King, to complete the work of Cão and Dias. This was Manuel's own view, but he wished it to be argued within the council, so that he would gain support from the grandees of the country, and when the whole of the council concurred, he felt free to proceed with his arrangements.

Bartolomeu Dias, who had been appointed to the staff of Guinea House in 1494, was named to supervise the construction of two *naus* specially designed under his direction for the next voyage of exploration. Pacheco Pereira described the building of these ships, into which Dias incorporated all the experience he had gained on his voyage.

'They were built by excellent masters and workmen, of strong nails and wood,' Pereira records; 'each ship had three sets of sails and anchors, and three or four times as much other tackle and rigging as was usual. The cooperage of the casks, pipes and barrels of wine, water, vinegar and oil was strengthened with many hoops of iron. The provisions of bread, wine, flour, meat, vegetables, medicines, and likewise of arms and ammunition, were also in excess of what was needed for such a voyage. The best and most skilful pilots and mariners in Portugal were sent on this voyage, and they received, besides other favours, salaries higher than those of other countries. The money spent on the few ships was so great that I will not go into detail for fear of not being believed.'

The two ships whose construction was supervised by Dias were each of about 200 modern tons displacement, square-rigged on two masts, with a lateen sail on the mizzen. Two other ships were bought, one of about 100 tons, and the other—intended to carry extra stores and provisions—of about 300 tons. It is significant of Portuguese social attitudes in the fifteenth century that the command of the vital expedition which it was hoped would finally establish Portuguese trade with the Indies should have been entrusted not to the commoner Dias, who had the greatest claims in terms of achievement, but to the *fidalgo* Vasco da Gama, a member of the noble class whose support was essential to Manuel in his expansionist activities.

Dias was instead appointed to the command of a vessel directed to the Guinea coast, and kept company with Vasco da Gama's squadron as far as the Cape Verde islands, where, as he took leave to make his solitary way to São Jorge de Mina, he must have watched the departing ships with a regret that was deepened not only by the fact that Vasco da Gama would be gaining a triumph based on his experience, but also by the presence in the squadron proceeding to the Indies of Pero de Alenquer who had served under him in the discovery of the Cape of Good Hope and Pero Escolar who had accompanied Cão up the Congo and as far as the Serra Parda.

The story of Vasco da Gama's voyage, which began when the squadron left the Tagus on July 1497 and attained its objective when da Gama's ships anchored off Calicut in

Malabar in May the following year, is too well known to justify repetition here. It is sufficient to say that in the earlier part of his voyage Vasco da Gama profited by the knowledge of the coastline and the prevalent Atlantic winds that Cão and Dias had accumulated, just as in the Indian Ocean he took advantage of the knowledge of Arab pilots, and especially of Ibn Majid, provided by the sultan of Malindi who accepted the Portuguese as allies in order to satisfy his hostility to the rival sultan of Mombasa.

Meanwhile, after seeing da Gama's squadron depart on its way to India, Bartolomeu Dias sailed to the coast of Guinea. He transported a cargo of trade-goods to Mina, and brought back gold and slaves which were sold to provide the finances for further expeditions. He must have acquired a certain expertise in the gold trade, since when Vasco da Gama returned to Portugal in 1499 with information regarding the gold trade of the east African coast, King Manuel selected Dias to found a fortress-factory, similar to São Jorge de Mina, at the gold-exporting port of Sofala.

When the Portuguese reached East Africa this trade was in the hands of Muslims who travelled inland, accompanied by porters bearing beads and Indian cloths, from the sheikh's village which was set among coconut palms and baobab trees on what was then the wide estuary of the Revue River. Accompanied by dugout canoes which carried some of their trade-goods the Muslims followed the course of the river to the end of navigation and then struck across the sandy coastal plain to the highlands of Manica, whence they reached the lands of the Karanga tribe in the northern part of modern Rhodesia, where Monomotpapa was the paramount chief. The traders visited local fairs wherever there was gold to be bartered, and travelled as far as the middle reaches of the Zambesi, where they traded with caravans that came down from Katanga with copper ingots in the shape of St. Andrew's crosses. All this trade was soon to be described by a Portuguese, António Fernandes, who visited these areas between 1511 and 1514. But in 1499 it was still only the gold trade that attracted Portuguese attention to Sofala.

Manuel decided to send a strong armada to the Indian Ocean in order to take advantage of Vasco da Gama's discoveries. The sixteenth-century chroniclers, probably imitating each other, agree that there were thirteen vessels in the fleet, but documentary sources closer to the event give figures varying between twelve and fourteen. However, it is certain that part of the armada was a squadron of four ships under the command of Bartolomeu Dias; they were all caravels, because of the shallow waters at Sofala and off the coast northward in the direction of Moçambique.

The fleet as a whole was commanded by Pedro Álvares Cabral. It assembled off Restelo at the mouth of the Tagus at the beginning of March 1500, and on the 8th of that month King Manuel and the crews of all the ships attended a mass in a local chapel. It was only, however, on the afternoon of the 9th March that sufficient wind sprang up for them to make their departure. On the 18th March they sighted the Canaries, and on the 22nd they came to the Cape Verde islands, to find that one vessel had been lost; it was never seen again.

Since there was no need for this fleet to follow the coast of Africa as Cão and Dias had done, Vasco da Gama had provided Cabral with instructions as to the best route down the Atlantic. From the Cape Verde islands he recommended him to sail southward, with the north-east trade winds astern. Once across the doldrums he should steer south-westward, to take advantage of the south-east trade winds, and then, sailing as close to the wind as possible, he should make southing until he could approach the Cape of Good Hope on an easting. As Admiral Morison remarked in *Portuguese Voyages to America in the Fifteenth Century*, these instructions 'testify to the careful observations of da Gama, of Dias and of the generation of Portuguese navigators that preceded them in Guinea voyages'; moreover, in 1498 Pacheco Pereira may well have explored farther into the Atlantic than any of the voyagers we have so far discussed.

In fact, Cabral's route took him, perhaps intentionally, farther to the west than any previous Portuguese voyagers, and it seems likely that in secret instructions he was commanded to begin his journey by exploring what might lie in the Atlantic along the western edge of the area allotted to Portugal under the Treaty of Tordesillas—i.e. the area terminated by an imaginary line 370 leagues west of the Cape Verde islands. It was thus, in April 1500, that Brazil was first discovered.

On the 21st of that month the crews of the fleet saw seaweed floating beside their ships; the next morning they saw birds, and at evening on the 22nd April they sighted land; it was Monte Pascoal, a remarkable peak, 1,760 feet high which, according to the *South American Pilot*, 'may be seen at a great distance, and from its height and isolation is a most useful landmark for this part of the coast'. Since it was Holy Week, Cabral called this land the Terra da Vera Cruz, and at sunset he ordered the fleet to anchor, in nineteen fathoms, six leagues from the shore. The next day the fleet spread sail and made for land, with the smaller vessels, including the squadron commanded by Dias, in the lead. They anchored half a league from shore, in nine fathoms.

Cabral now ordered Coelho, who had commanded the

smallest of Vasco da Gama's ships, to reconnoitre in his longboat. As soon as it reached the beach, a score of the local people appeared. They were swarthy in colour, entirely naked, and they carried bows and arrows. Coelho threw them three hats, and they threw him a head-dress covered in feathers.

That night a strong south-easterly wind blew up and the ships dragged anchor. The following morning conditions were still unpleasant, and though seventy natives appeared on the shore, Cabral ordered anchors to be weighed and the vessels sailed ten leagues down wind to the north where the smaller vessels found a projecting point of coral and secure anchorage in its lee. A league off this point, at sundown, the vessels anchored. A pilot, ordered to sound the harbour, ran close to land and took prisoner two men in a dugout canoe who, according to the description of an eye-witness, Vaz de Caminha, 'are of a darkish, slightly reddish colour. They have good features and well-shaped noses. They go about absolutely naked, without any covering. They care no more about covering up their private parts than their faces. They are very innocent in this matter. They both had holes in their lower lip and a bone in them as big as the breadth of a hand, as thick as a cotton spindle and sharp at the end like a bodkin. They put these in from within the lip, and the part which remains between the lip and the teeth is made like a rook at chess. And they fit them in such a way that they do not hurt them or prevent them from talking or eating or drinking. Their hairs are straight.' One of the captives pointed at Cabral's golden collar and at a silver candlestick, and then at the land, which the Portuguese took as a sure sign that it contained gold and silver.

The following morning the vessels spread sail, edged close towards the land, and anchored in five or six fathoms.

So large and secure was the anchorage that two hundred vessels could have sheltered in safety in this Porto Seguro (the present Baía Cabrália), as Vaz de Caminha reported to his monarch. Cabral called the captains to his flagship, and ordered Coelho and Bartolomeu Dias to take the two captives ashore and set them free. Their bows and arrows were restored to them, and each was given a new shirt, a red cap, and a rosary of white bone beads and little bells. Cabral also ordered that a convict, a young man sentenced to exile, should be put ashore with instructions to learn the customs of the people.

Over 200 men were on the beach when they landed. The two men who had been abducted leapt away across the Mutari River, but soon they returned without their caps, and the natives brought back the young convict. Bartolomeu Dias ordered him to return and hand some presents to an elderly man who had befriended him, and this he did, but afterwards rejoined his compatriots. More and more people appeared, and among them were three or four young and attractive girls with long black hair who were completely unashamed in their nudity. One of them was dyed with some colouring matter from head to toe; Vaz de Caminha commented that she was so well shaped and rounded, and her lack of shame was so delightful, that many Portuguese ladies might well have envied her.

The Portuguese returned, and mass was celebrated on the low islet of Coroa Vermelha at the tip of the point, beneath the banner bearing the cross of Christ which King Manuel had presented to Cabral at Restelo. Then they re-embarked and made for the shore, which was now crowded with the native people. Cabral ordered Bartolomeu Dias to go first and test their mood. Before stepping ashore from his long-boat, Dias made signs to the warriors that they should put down their bows and arrows, and this they did, except for one who appeared to be a leader of some kind, though he was treated with little respect by his fellows; he differed from them in being dyed all over with a red pigment which the seawater did not remove, but merely seemed to intensify.

A seaman now jumped out of Dias's boat, and went among the people. They did not harm him; instead, they offered him a gourd of water to drink from and gestured to the others to come ashore. Dias, however, returned to Cabral and reported on the friendliness of the natives. After dinner Cabral called a council, attended by Dias and the other captains and officers, at which it was decided to send the storeship back to Portugal with news of the discovery of this new land. Cabral then suggested that they might kidnap two of the natives and send them to King Manuel, leaving two convicts in their places to learn the local language and gather information about the country. More pacific counsels, however, prevailed. 'Let us not think of taking anybody by force or of causing scandal,' it was decided. 'Rather let us conciliate and pacify them and merely leave two exiles when we go.'

The Portuguese now went ashore, with Cabral at their head. The natives crowded around him, among them braves painted in red and black and a number of women. 'They who were young, being nude, did not look bad,' Vaz de Caminha remarked. 'One of them had a thigh dyed entirely in black from the knee past the buttocks to the hip, while all the rest of her was the natural colour. Another had both the backs of her knees and the ankles of her feet dyed; and her private parts so naked and with such uncovered innocence that there was no immodesty in this.'

Beyond the river many of the natives were dancing and rejoicing. Diogo Dias, Bartolomeu's handsome and lively brother, crossed over with a bagpiper and danced with them; he performed many light turns and a somersault, which greatly amused them, until suddenly and inexplicably they took fright, like wild creatures from the hills, and flitted away. Bartolomeu Dias must have been fascinated by the contrast between the appearance and behaviour of these South Americans and those of the negroes with whom he had dealt on the Guinea coast and the Hottentots he had encountered in southern Africa.

Cabral and his companions crossed the river, and continued along the spit of land between the sea and the lagoon. Dias had killed a shark, and this was presented to a group of natives who appeared; they accepted it, but then threw it down on the beach. Cabral ordered three of the convicts condemned to banishment to spend the night with the local people, and he sent Diogo Dias with them, 'since he was a merry fellow and knew how to amuse them'. Diogo and the exiles accompanied the people to their village a league and a half away. It consisted of nine or ten high wooden houses, with no partitions but with hammocks stretched from pole to pole; each house contained a community of thirty or forty people. They refused to allow the Portuguese to stay overnight.

The Portuguese raised a timber cross and celebrated mass while 400 or 500 natives assembled on the beach, 'so healthy and well-shaped and gallant in their paint', Vaz de Caminha remembered, 'that it was a pleasure to see them'. Cabral and his fleet departed on the 2nd May 1500. It is significant that Vaz de Caminha makes no reference to the erection of a *padrão*, and that none is mentioned in the letter which King Manuel wrote to his royal cousins in Spain, Ferdinand and Isabella, telling them of the achievements of Cabral's voyage. This omission tends to prove that it was not—as some historians have contended—an official assertion of sovereignty over a coastline already discovered before Cabral's arrival. Had this been the case, King Manuel would certainly have provided Cabral with a stone *padrão* to erect as a permanent monument. Thus we can fairly assume that Bartolomeu Dias was an active participant in the first discovery of Brazil.

But this was to be his last achievement. On the 12th May a large comet with a long tail appeared in the sky, apparently over the Cape of Good Hope towards which the fleet was making, and for eight days it hung there in the sky without apparent movement. 'It seemed', remarked Barros, 'to be a prognostication of the sad event that was to take place.' On the 23rd May the comet disappeared, and on the same day the sea began to run high. On the 24th May, after midday, there appeared in the sky to the north a black cloud of a type well known to mariners accustomed to the Guinea coast. The wind dropped, as though the cloud were absorbing it, Barros declared, only to discharge it in most furious strength.

'This happened suddenly: the wind burst down in an instant so furiously that there was no time for the seamen to work the sails, and four vessels were overwhelmed, the captains of which were Aires Gomes de Silva, Simão de Pina, Vasco de Taide and Bartolomeu Dias. The last had passed so many dangers at sea in the discoveries he had made, and principally of the Cabo da Boa Esperança (as we have described above) but this fury of wind ended his life and those of others, casting them into the great abyss of that ocean sea which that day smote all of us, and giving human bodies as food for the fishes of those seas . . .'

The remaining ships kept afloat, but the survivors were sorely tried. 'Though the action of this blast of wind was the most terrifying thing that any of them had seen, and came close to others being miserably lost, yet they were even more terrified at seeing above them the darkest night: the blackness of the weather spread all over the sky in such a way that they could not see, nor could they hear for the raging of the wind. At times they could feel the fury of the seas propelling the ships so fast upon the crests of the waves that it seemed as though they would be launched out of the sea and into the air; and at others it suddenly seemed as if they would be engulfed and buried in the abyss of earth. In the end the fear of these things sapped the courage of all men, so that most of the mariners could do no more than call on the name of Jesus and his Mother, begging pardon for their sins, which is the last word of those who are in the presence of death. And with the fury of the sea and the weakness of the seamen the ships were driven at the will of the winds without help of helm.'

One ship was blown alongside another, and it seemed that their mutual destruction was inevitable, but the next blast separated them, and they were saved. But for twenty days the surviving ships were driven along under bare masts, for the wind tore away the smallest shred of sail. Eventually Cabral found himself off Sofala with only six ships, and those stripped of sail. Diogo Dias had lost company with the fleet, but he was safe; he reached the north-east coast of Africa and explored the entrance to the Red Sea.

After the death of Bartolomeu Dias and the loss of so many ships, it was impossible on this voyage to establish a post at Sofala. Cabral sailed on to Calicut where he established a trading factory, but the Muslims destroyed this (Vaz de Caminha was among those killed) and Cabral bombarded the city and seized Muslim ships in revenge. At Cochin, however, he succeeded in trading for spices and establishing what became a lasting relationship between the Portuguese and the local raja, while in Cannanore, to the north of Calicut, he persuaded the ruler to send an ambassador back with him to Portugal. These alliances meant that the Portuguese sea route to India was finally assured, with the most profound historical consequences for both the Eastern and the Western Worlds. In the establishment of that route between Europe and the Indies the explorations of Cão and Dias had been decisive.

Selected Bibliography

a) BOOKS

Africa Pilot, Part II, including the West coast of Africa, from Rio del Rey to False Bay . . ., Hydrographic Department, Admiralty, London, e.g. 1922. An indispensable aid for the appearance of the coast, currents and depth of water and climate. The same comment applies to *The African Pilot, Part III, South and East coasts of Africa from Table Bay to Ras Hafún*, Hydrographic Department, Admiralty, London, e.g. 1929.

ALBUQUERQUE, Luís Mendonça de, *Os guias náuticos de Munique e Évora*, Agrupamento de Estudos de Cartografia Antiga, 4, Secção de Coimbra, Lisbon, 1965. Useful for knowing the saints' days familiar to pilots of the late fifteenth century.

AXELSON, E., *South-East Africa 1488-1530*, London, 1940.

——, *Portuguese in South-East Africa, 1488-1600*, Cape Town, 1973.

BAGROW, L., *History of Cartography*, revised and enlarged by R. A. Skelton, London, 1964.

BAIÃO, A., *et al.*, *História da expansão Portuguesa no Mundo*, Lisbon, 1937.

BALANDIER, G., *Daily Life in the Kingdom of the Kongo*, London, 1968.

BARBOSA, A., *Novos subsídios para a história da ciência náutica portuguesa da época dos descobrimentos*, Oporto, 1948.

BARROS, João, *Asia . . . Primeira decada*, ed. António Baião, Coimbra, 1930. This volume of the great chronicler was completed in 1539 and first published in 1552.

BECKINGHAM, C. F., and G. W. B. HUNTINGFORD, eds., *The Prester John of the Indies: a true relation of the lands of the Prester John being the narrative of the Portuguese Embassy to Ethiopia in 1520, written by Father Francisco Alvares*, 2 vols., Hakluyt Society, Cambridge, 1961. Contains information of Pero da Covilhã.

BLAKE, J. W., *Europeans in West Africa, 1454-1578*, London, 1937.

BOVILL, E. W., *The Golden Trade of the Moors*, 2nd ed. Robin Hallett, London, 1968.

BOXER, C. R., *The Portuguese Seaborne Empire 1415-1825*, London, 1969.

BRÁSIO, António, *Monumenta Missionaria Africana África Ocidental (1342–1499)*, Segunda Serie I, Lisbon, 1958.

CAMPOS, Viriato, *Viagens de Diogo Cão e de Bartolomeu Dias*, Lisbon, 1966. Contains some stimulating suggestions.

CASTANHEDA, Fernão Lopes de, *História do descobrimento e conquista da India pelos portugueses*, I, Coimbra, 1924. Castanheda was usually the most accurate of the chroniclers; but he had little to say on Cão and Dias.

CORTESÃO, Armando, *Cartografia e cartógrafos portugueses dos seculos XV e XVI*, 2 vols., Lisbon, 1935.

——, *History of Portuguese Cartography* I, Coimbra, 1969. It includes a chapter, 'The greatest hoax in the history of geography: the legend of Prester John'.

——, and Avelino Teixeira da MOTA, *Portugaliae Monumenta Cartografica*, vols. I and II, Lisbon, 1960. A truly monumental work.

——, Jaime, *Os descobrimentos Portugueses*, 2 vols., Lisbon, no date.

COSTA, A. Fontoura da, *A marinharia dos descobrimentos*, Lisbon, 1960.

——, *Os sete únicos documentos de 1500, conservados em Lisboa, referentes à viagen de Pedro Álvares Cabral*, Lisbon, 1940. Contains the letter by Vaz de Caminha.

COSTA, A. Fontoura da, ed., *Roteiro da África do sul e sueste desde o Cabo da Boa Esperança até ao das Correntes (1576) por Manuel de Mesquita Perestrelo*, Lisbon, 1939.

COUTINHO, Gago, *A náutica dos descobrimentos*, 2 vols., Lisbon, 1951.

CRAWFORD, O. G. S., *Ethiopian Itineraries circa 1400–1524*, Hakluyt Society, Cambridge, 1958.

CRONE, G. R., *Maps and their Makers*, London, 1968.

DINIS, António J. Dias, *Vida e obras de Gomes Eanes de Zurara*, 2 vols., Lisbon, 1949.

FICALHO, Conde de, *Viagens de Pedro da Covilham*, Lisbon, 1898.

GARCIA, Carlos Alberto, *Do Cabo Sta Catarina à Serra Parda ...*, Lisbon, 1971.

GODINHO, Vitorino Magalhães, *Documentos sobre a expansão portuguesa*, 3 vols., Lisbon, [?–1956].

——, *Os descobrimentos e a economia mundial*, 2 vols., [1963–71].

GREENLEE, W. B., ed. and trans., *The Voyage of Pedro Álvares Cabral to Brazil and India from Contemporary Documents and Narratives*, Hakluyt Society, London, 1937.

HAMAN, Günther, *Der Eintritt der Südlichen Hemisphäre in die Europäische Geschichte: Die Erschliessung des Afrikaweges nach Asien vom Zeitalten Heinrichs des Seefahrers bis zu Vasco da Gama*, Vienna, 1968.

HENNIG, R., *Terrae Incognitae*, Leiden, 4 vols., 1936–9.

História da Colonização portuguesa do Brasil, II, Oporto, 1921.

LEITE, Duarte, *História dos descobrimentos*, ed. V. Magalhães Godinho, Lisbon, 1958.

LETTS, Malcolm, *Mandeville's Travels*, II, Hakluyt Society, London, 1953.

LEY, C. D., *Portuguese Voyages 1498–1663*, London, 1947. Includes a translation of the Vaz de Caminha letter.

LISBOA, João de, J. I. de Brito Rebello, ed., *Livro de marinharia: tratado da agulha de marear de João de Lisboa*, Lisbon, 1903. The rutter attached contains a detailed description of the South African coast.

LIVERMORE, H. V., *A History of Portugal*, Cambridge, 1947.

MAUNY, R., *Les navigations médiévales sur les côtes sahariennes antérieures à la découverte portugaise (1434)*, Lisbon, 1960.

MORISON, Samuel E., *Portuguese Voyages to America in the Fifteenth Century*, Cambridge, Mass., 1940.

——, *Admiral of the Ocean Sea*, Boston, 1942.

MOTA, Avelino Teixeira da, *Bartolomeu Dias Discoverer of Cape of Good Hope*, Lisbon, 1955.

PEREIRA, Duarte Pacheco, *Esmeraldo de Situ Orbis*, ed. A. E. da Silva Dias, Lisbon, 1905. With a description of the west coast of Africa and the south coast as far as the Infante River.

——, *Esmeraldo de Situ Orbis*, trans. and ed. G. H. T. Kimble, Hakluyt Society, London, 1937.

PERES, Damião, *História dos descobrimentos portugueses*, Oporto, 1943. Still the most comprehensive and authoritative work on the Portuguese discoveries.

——, *Diogo Cão*, Lisbon, 1957.

——, *Diogo Cão*, English trans. by M. Freire de Andrade, Lisbon, 1957.

——, *Diário da Viagem de Vasco da Gama*, I, Oporto, 1945. By Álvaro Velho.

PERESTRÊLO, Manuel de Mesquita, see Costa, A. Fontoura da.

PIGAFETTA, Filippo, *A Report of The Kingdom of Congo . . . Duarte Lopez*, trans. and ed. by Margarite Hutchinson, London, 1881, reprinted 1970.

PINA, Rui de, *Chrónica de el-Rey D. Duarte*, Oporto, 1914.

——, Rui de, *Chrónica de el-Rei D. Afonso V*, Lisbon, 1902.

——, *Croniqua del Rey Dom Joham II*, Coimbra, 1950.

PRESTAGE, Edgar, *The Portuguese Pioneers*, London, 1933. A pioneer work.

RAVENSTEIN, E. G., *Martin Behaim, his Life and his Globe*, London, 1908.

RESENDE, Garcia de, *Chrónica de el-rei D. João II*, Lisbon, 1902.

ROGERS, Francis, *The Quest for Eastern Christians*, Minneapolis, 1962.

TAYLOR, E. G. R., *The Haven-Finding Art*, London, 1956.

[VELHO, Álvaro], see Peres, Damião, *Diario . . .*

SELECTED BIBLIOGRAPHY

ZURARA, Gomes Eanes da, *Crónica da tomada de Ceuta*, Lisbon, 1915.

——, *Crónica do Conde Dom Pedro de Menezes* . . ., Lisbon, 1792.

——, *Crónica dos feitos de Guiné*, see Dinis, A. J. Dias.

——, *The Chronicle of the Discovery and Conquest of Guinea* . . ., trans. by C. R. Beazley and Edgar Prestage, 2 vols., Hakluyt Society, London, 1896, 1899.

b) ARTICLES, OFFPRINTS AND PAMPHLETS

ALBUQUERQUE, Luís Mendonça de, 'O primeira guia náutico português e o problema das latitudes na marinha dos séculos XV e XVI', offprint from *Revista da Universidade de Coimbra*, 19, 1960.

——, and J. Lopes TAVARES, 'Algumas observações sobre o planisfério "Cantino" (1502)', offprint from *Revista da Universidade de Coimbra*, 1967, Agrupamento de Estudos de Cartografia Antiga, XXI, Secção de Coimbra, 1967.

AXELSON, E., 'Discovery of the Farthest Pillar Erected by Bartholomew Dias', *South African Journal of Science*, Dec. 1938, pp. 417–29.

——, 'O padrão da Angra das Voltas', *Boletim da Sociedade de Geografia de Lisboa*, January–March 1955, pp. 23–31.

——, 'Prince Henry the Navigator and the Discovery of the Sea-route to India', *Geographical Journal*, June 1961, pp. 145–58.

BAGROW, L., 'The Wilczek–Brown Codex', *Imago Mundi* XII, 1955, pp. 171–4.

BECKINGHAM, C. F., 'The Travels of Pero da Covilhã and their Significance', Congresso Internacional de História dos Descobrimentos, *Actas* II, Lisbon, 1961, pp. 1–14.

BRAZ, C. S. Moura, 'Subsídios para um roteiro da costa de Angola', *Anais* do Club Militar Naval, 1937, pp. 21–157.

CAMPOS, Viriato, *O ancoradouro secreto da nau de mantimentos da frota descobridora do Cabo*, Lisbon, 1966 (pamphlet).

CASTILHO, Alexandre Magno de, 'Os padrões dos descobrimentos Portugueses em África', *Memórias* da Academia Real das Sciencias de Lisboa, IV, part 1, 1869.

——, 'Os padrões dos descobrimentos Portugueses em África', Segunda memória, ib., 1871.

CASTRO, A. C. da Silva, 'Diogo Cão e a legenda de Henrique Martelo', Congresso Internacional de História dos Descobrimentos, *Actas* II, Lisbon, 1961, pp. 85–106.

CORDEIRO, Luciano, 'O ultimo padrão de Diogo Cão', *Boletim da Sociedade de Geografia de Lisboa*, 1895, pp. 885–94.

COSTA, A. Fontoura da, 'Às portas da India em 1484', offprint from

Anais do Club Militar Naval, Lisbon, 1935. A most substantial and valuable work of 124 pages.

——, 'S. Gregório em False Island, como afirmei em 1935', *Memórias da Academia das Ciências de Lisboa, Classe da Cetras*, III, Lisbon, 1938, pp. 1–13.

CRONE, G. R., 'Martin Behaim, Navigator and Cosmographer: Figment of Imagination or Historical Personage?', Congresso Internacional da História dos descobrimentos, *Actas II*, Lisbon, 1961, pp. 117–33.

DENNETT, R. E., 'Discovery of One of Diego Cam's Pillars at Shark's Point, Congo', *Journal of the Manchester Geographical Society*, III, 1887, pp. 122–3.

FARIA, Francisco Leito de, 'Uma relação de Rui de Pina sobre o Congo escrita em 1492', *Stvdia* 19, Dec. 1966, pp. 223–304, and offprint, Agrupamento de Estudos de Cartografia Antiga, XVIII, Secção de Lisboa, Lisbon, 1966.

MOTA, A. Teixeira da, 'A viagem de Bartolomeu Dias e as concepções geopolíticas de D. João II', *Boletim* da Sociedade de Geografia de Lisboa, Oct.–Dec. 1958, pp. 297–322.

——, 'A evolução da Ciência náutica durante os séculos XV–XVI na cartografia Portuguesa da época', offprint from *Memórias* da Academia das Ciências de Lisboa—Classe de Letras, VII, 1961, Agrupamento de Estudos de Cartografia Antiga, III, Secção de Lisboa, 1961.

RAVENSTEIN, E. G., 'The Voyages of Diogo Cão and Bartholomew Dias, 1482–88', *Geographical Journal*, 1900, pp. 625–55. A most important work, with valuable identifications of cartographical references.

SKELTON, R. A., 'An Ethiopian Embassy to Western Europe in 1306', Appendix in O. G. S. Crawford, *Ethiopian Itineraries circa 1400–1524*, q.v.

WATERS, D. W., 'Science and the Techniques of Navigation', in C. S. Singleton, ed., *Art, Science and History in the Renaissance*, Baltimore, 1967.

Index

213